AMERICAN
GRIT

AMERICAN
GRIT

WHAT IT WILL TAKE TO SURVIVE
AND WIN IN THE 21ST CENTURY

TONY BLANKLEY

AUTHOR OF *THE WEST'S LAST CHANCE*

Since 1947
REGNERY
PUBLISHING, INC.
An Eagle Publishing Company • Washington, DC

Cataloging-in-Publication data on file with the Library of Congress

ISBN 978-1-59698-519-3

Published in the United States by
Regnery Publishing, Inc.
One Massachusetts Avenue, NW
Washington, DC 20001
www.regnery.com

Manufactured in the United States of America
10 9 8 7 6 5 4 3 2 1

Books are available in quantity for promotional or premium use. Write to Director of Special Sales, Regnery Publishing, Inc., One Massachusetts Avenue NW, Washington, DC 20001, for information on discounts and terms or call (202) 216-0600.

To our three children who we love so dearly, Trevor, Ana, and Spencer: May they—and all our country's children—continue to commit their strength and intelligence to the cause of keeping America strong and free.

CONTENTS

★ ★ ★

CHAPTER ONE

THE CASE FOR
A NEW AMERICAN
NATIONALISM

THESE ARE DANGEROUS DAYS FOR OUR COUNTRY. WE FACE ENOR-
mous challenges at home and gathering threats from abroad.
And just when the situation requires us to return to the proven traditions of our history, our government is led by a man, Barack
Obama, and a Democratic Party that are seized of all the wrong values and policies for such a national struggle.

At a time of economic crisis we have a government run by a man
who wants to adopt socialistic tax and spending policies to "spread
the wealth"—policies that will severely weaken our economy's productive capacity. This capacity will be further damaged by President
Obama's energy policies, which will hinder efficient energy production in furtherance of the chimera of absolute environmental purity.
As our economic dominance is increasingly challenged by the looming economic giants of China, India, and even Brazil, our president

opposes free trade and voices suspicion of private enterprise, which are the tools that give our economy its competitive edge.

At a time when Iran, one of the chief international sponsors of Islamic terrorism, draws closer every day to gaining possession of weapons of mass destruction, our foreign policy is being run by someone who believes that Mahmoud Ahmadinejad—an Islamist of dubious sanity who denies the Holocaust, threatens to obliterate Israel, and is racing to develop nuclear weapons—is a leader we can talk to. With the Russians threatening to place missiles next to Poland, with North Korea still threatening nuclear proliferation, with the nuclear Islamic state of Pakistan in turmoil, with an ongoing global war against Islamist terrorists, and with anti-American regimes solidifying their power in Latin America, President Obama shows more concern for stopping the effective surveillance of terrorism suspects and protecting the "rights" of captured enemy combatants than for defending our national security.

At a time when our national unity is fraying and when the American people are dividing themselves into competing identity groups with an increasingly tenuous sense of collective destiny, our nation's leader refuses to call for patriotic sacrifice for the good of the country. Instead, he promises only to further expand our ever-growing entitlements.

On these three crucial issues—the economy, national security, and national unity—the United States faces critical challenges. As this book went to press, these dangers were brought home in a stark report released by the National Intelligence Council. In it, our top intelligence agencies predicted the coming decline of America's dominance of global affairs. The next two decades, the report found, will likely be characterized by wars over natural resources, a growing number of rogue states, dire threats from nuclear proliferation, and the end of the dollar's position as the world's primary currency.[1]

Just after the report's release, a horrific Islamic terrorist attack in Mumbai, India left nearly 200 people dead, providing a grim reminder of the lurking danger that threatens every democracy.

President Obama campaigned on promises of "hope" and "change." But these are not the most pressing issues of the moment. Our biggest concern, in fact, is our national survival.

SHIFTING WINDS

Americans have repeatedly overcome serious adversities, but in the past we've had the wind of history at our back. For two centuries no nation on earth could match our combination of land, natural resources, and our free, disciplined, industrious, religious, productive, and entrepreneurial people.

Empowered by our many blessings, we Americans have always had the luxury of a wide margin for error. We have thrived despite episodic bad policy from Washington, ill-conceived wars, counterproductive educational and social policies, excessive taxes, natural disasters, and even the occasional madness of our collective judgment. Our endurance was enabled by our uncanny sense of balance between the prerogatives of the individual and the need for collective sacrifice and action.

Up until World War II we were masters of our fate within our lands. While we traded with the world, we didn't need the world—and the world could do little to us. And for a long half century after the war our economic, military, diplomatic, cultural, and political strength assured us a smooth passage through history. Two poorly judged, and embarrassingly ended, wars in Asia (Korea and Vietnam) barely left a ripple of adversity in our postwar foreign affairs. So strong were we, we could afford to get bloodied in war and yet maintain our global preeminence.

But now the magnitudes work against us.

We once developed our own vast energy supplies. Now we rely on foreign oil, sending almost a trillion dollars a year to Middle Eastern countries that use their oil money to fund the Islamist war of terror against us. This debilitating dependence has sucked us into the religious, tribal, and national struggles and wars of the Middle East. The day will probably come, if we don't quickly change things, when we will no longer fight to protect friendly regimes but will have to seize, hold, extract, and export the oil we need.

During wartime, we traditionally have fielded well-staffed armies big enough to overwhelm our enemies. Now, the military has shrunk to a level that seriously threatens our ability to respond to international crises.

We used to band together during threatening times, putting the country first. Now, the idea of personal sacrifice is absent from public discussion. Even the horror of the September 11 attacks was not enough to galvanize our leaders into asking Americans to shake off their complacency and personally contribute to the country's security.

All these challenges have led me to reconsider what principles of governance are best suited to overcome the dangers before us. In my previous book, *The West's Last Chance: Will We Win the Clash of Civilizations?*, I argued that America cannot become strong enough to win the war on Islamic terrorism by following the strict libertarian principles I believed in before and during my years on Ronald Reagan's White House staff.

But it never occurred to me precisely where my political philosophy was moving until an appearance on the *McLaughlin Group* television show a few years ago. During one of our fierce debates about the Iraq War, John McLaughlin turned to me and asked "What do you neo-cons want?" I responded pugnaciously, "I'm not a neo-con," to which John reasonably inquired, "Well what are you?" With the red light of the television camera focused on me, I paused and thought for a second or two, and then more or less blurted out, "I'm a nationalist!"

That ended the conversation, but only started me thinking more about my answer. Was it the right answer? Am I a nationalist? What does that mean in America in the twenty-first century?

I still emphatically characterize myself as a conservative. But as one goes through the various zoological categories of the breed— neo, paleo, social, traditional, cultural, free market—none of them quite captures the driving thrust of my views these days.

What I have come to realize is that whether it is on issues of trade, legal theory, war fighting, economics, the environment, educational practices, energy production, or foreign policy—while I usually fall upon conservative policy prescriptions, my motive is this: What will help America? What will make her strong and safe? My first objective is no longer to find the policy that best fits my definition of conservative, but rather to find the surest path to protecting my country. Usually they coincide—but not always.

For example, I am completely for free markets. However, since the free market cannot produce energy independence for America fast enough, I support government programs such as price guarantees to assure energy independence. So I am for the nation before I am for pure laissez faire principles—although I strongly favor economic freedom wherever possible.

I think of Abraham Lincoln's powerful commitment to the Union. In 1862, as the Civil War raged and the Confederacy was getting the better of the North, Lincoln wrote: "My paramount object in this struggle *is* to save the Union, and is *not* either to save or to destroy slavery. If I could save the Union without freeing *any* slave I would do it, and if I could save it by freeing *all* the slaves I would do it; and if I could save it by freeing some and leaving others alone I would also do that. What I do about slavery, and the colored race, I do because I believe it helps to save the Union."[2]

Of course, Lincoln despised slavery and wanted it abolished, but he was completely committed to saving the Union, even above honoring her best principle (freedom) or defeating her worst conduct (slavery). I share Lincoln's instinct, which I believe is still the instinct of most Americans: that America was and remains the last best hope of mankind. So long as America is strong and free, the upward trajectory of man is still possible—and indeed is still underway. Without America to give hope to all of man's nobler instincts, what a cruel, nasty place the world would be.

So to hope for American strength is to hope for the safety of all mankind, to hope for the triumph of decency and freedom.

It is with that in mind that I support the no longer popular proposition, "May my country always be right, but my country right or wrong." Long considered a jingoistic embarrassment of a slogan, it shouldn't be. America will always make mistakes, but more important is this: in our world, only America—a militarily, economically, and culturally dominant America—can stand and fight for things worth standing and fighting for. If America falls from its position of dominance, there will be no power on earth left to check the advance of tyranny and suffering and despair.

STRENGTH AND SACRIFICE

Patriotism is love for one's country; nationalism is a call to action, a commitment to make difficult decisions on behalf of what will make America strong—both spiritually and materially—even at the expense of what might make us momentarily more comfortable. A nationalist recognizes that each citizen owes the country something.

If the country is in danger, then we must be prepared to subordinate our individual wants for the national interest.

Now let me be clear: America's greatest strength, the reason we are the exceptional country on the planet, the reason we provide hope for mankind, the reason America is worth sacrificing for, is precisely that America is the land of individual freedom—both personal and economic.

These days, however, too many people confuse individual freedom with the mere right to live in a geographical area called the United States and do whatever they want with no care for the greater good. Citizenship is a two-way street: in exchange for the benefits of American freedom we are obliged to practice the virtues that make freedom possible. As stirringly rendered in "America the Beautiful," it means to confirm our souls in self-control, to seek liberty in law, to love country more than self, and to share the patriot's dream that sees beyond the years.

Nationalism must offer different prescriptions for different times. In the nineteenth century it meant accepting the dream of manifest destiny and building a continental nation. After World War II it meant bringing full freedom to black Americans who for far too long had been denied their full rights of citizenship and equality before the law.

Today, President Obama is set to implement an agenda that adheres to the precise opposite values than those held by a nationalist. His plans, characterized by economic redistributionism, environmentalism, well-intentioned diplomacy from weakness, and military retreat, promote national weakness as a cardinal virtue. Whether dealing with the economy, national security, or national unity, Obama's agenda takes human emotions—sensitivity, empathy, and self-satisfaction—and elevates them into national policy.

What I advocate in this book is a program based on a different set of values—toughness, resoluteness, and sacrifice—that have helped America persevere through world wars and economic depression, and would likewise see us through these trying times. A nationalist program, such as I propose, seeks to restore America's prosperity, military strength, and sense of patriotism. Above all else, it places the interests of the country first, even though that concept has fallen out of favor in recent years.

Currently, the best interest of the nation requires us to consider rolling back our attachment to personal rights and entitlements, an attachment that has become self-indulgent. Instead, in this time of foreign war and economic crisis, we need to become reacquainted with the American tradition of personal sacrifice for the good of the country.

For example, we can ill-afford the array of New Deal and Great Society entitlement programs that threaten to bankrupt our economy even before they are enlarged by the Obama administration. Is it in our national interest to short change the education of our youth, the building of needed infrastructure, the funding of vital research in science, the development of essential energy sources, and the maintenance of a military sufficient to assure our safety and dominance in the world, in order to continue funding such unsustainable programs as Medicare and Social Security? Even as a man who in a few short years will be eligible (and may well need) Medicare, I believe that a very hard decision will have to be made to truncate subsidized health care services to the old.

Personal sacrifice cannot be limited to the elderly, of course. The time for coddling our young adults must come to an end. America desperately needs their service in our dangerously short-handed military, which is so thinly stretched that top military officials now doubt our ability to respond if a new military crisis were to develop.

At various times throughout America's history, and for much of the twentieth century, American boys became men by shouldering the responsibility of serving in the military. This was a crucial rite of passage that benefited our country by keeping the army strong and cementing national unity. For these reasons and many others explained in chapter 2, I believe America should reinstitute the draft as part of a universal program of national service.

In sum, we should support certain state intrusions on personal freedom when they're necessary for the security of the country. This does not mean, however, that we should abide the effective abolition of free enterprise in favor of a centrally planned economy. Alas, there are disturbing signs that under President Obama we will be heading rapidly in this direction.

WAR ON THE FREE MARKET: COMING SOON TO A COUNTRY NEAR YOU

America has always benefited in a material and even spiritual way from free markets. The material benefits have been obvious, but the American work ethic, the willingness to take risks, and the sturdy sense of self-reliance are moral benefits that have shaped the American character. From time to time, however, historic events offer up a centralizing temptation to the American people. We face such a moment now. And instead of applying state power where it is vitally needed—to protect the homeland, defend national security secrets, increase our domestic energy supply, and replenish our military strength—the Obama administration looks set to ignore these pressing demands while it undertakes an all-out assault on the free market.

Having come of political age in 1962–63—the early days of the modern conservative, free market movement of Buckley, Goldwater, and Reagan—having seen the collapse of the Soviet Union and having witnessed the complete discrediting of the socialist experiment, I thought we had won that battle against the redistributors and public policy thieves of the left.

But time passes and people forget, and I suppose every generation is susceptible to the tempting argument that there is a free lunch, that the stern ethics and hard work required of citizens of free countries can be slackened without consequence, and that a public can sell out its economic freedoms for a mess of potage and still maintain the dignity that comes with being free and independent men and women.

Apparently, the public must learn again that the politicians who promise the fruits of other people's labor as inducement for votes are leading us down what the great economist F. A. Hayek called the "Road to Serfdom."

The new war on free markets was launched when a shocking financial panic hit America and the world in September 2008, a panic that understandably drove our government—and governments around the world—to immediate emergency action. As the world financial system seized up, central banks and ministers of finance shoveled unprecedented amounts of government money and credit into the system. Necessarily making it up as they went along—as stock exchanges plunged at historically unprecedented rates—governments adopted makeshift regulations and laws in a desperate effort to stave off financial and economic catastrophe.

Some semblance of normalcy has now returned—but the public fear lingers on. Middle class Americans have suffered severe losses in their stock portfolios while the value of their homes—the main source of equity for Americans—has also shrivelled. It is no overstatement to say that for the first time in their lives, many middle-class Americans have a genuine fear of having to face personal poverty—particularly for many who thought they were only a few years from comfortable retirement.

Predictably, just at such a moment the eternal enemies of free markets have seen their chance—and they are taking it.

We must appreciate the historical oddity of the system they are attacking. The embrace of freedom, whether legal, economic, or spiritual, is always an act of faith: a seemingly crazy belief that each individual can make his way through this baffling, dangerous world based on his own judgment alone. It is a world, moreover, where many of our fellow humans are as ravenous and unscrupulous as the wolves of our fairy tales.

That is why throughout history men have been offered the apparent safety of protection by strong men—if only they will relinquish their freedom. It is an offer that has usually been taken by a multitude taught to be fearful of this world. But once in a while in the tattered history of man, in a particular place, the squalid deal is rejected. For some strange reason a group of men decide to take their chances with freedom.

Such a time was 1776, and such a place was America. Fifty-six men declared their independence with the words: "And for the support of this Declaration with a firm reliance on the protection of divine providence, we mutually pledge to each other our lives, our fortunes, and our sacred honor."

But courage is a sometimes thing. Even the bravest man is not always brave. A free people sometimes devalue their birthright and are tempted by the eternal offer of surrender and safety. Of course, the strong men—or the men who aspire to be strong—offer their filthy deal when the people are the most vulnerable—as they feel now.

But even when a free people are afraid, the would-be strong men also use deception to try to win them over. So today, we hear the beguiling cry for big government, big regulations, and big taxes put forward by President Obama, the Democrats, and some Republicans. They argue that when even former President George W. Bush was prepared to nationalize the banks, there is really nothing left of free enterprise to defend. Of course, they deliberately fail to distinguish between emergency measures intended to reestablish conditions for the free market, and permanent policies designed to destroy the free market entirely.

The fall of the Soviet Union two decades ago deeply compromised the credibility and appeal of government-managed economies. As a result, throughout the world—and particularly in the United States—the past two decades have seen deregulation and a respect for markets flourish. Not only Marxists but also conventional big-government left-liberals in the West consistently lost the policy arguments to those of us who argued for a more vigorous, deregulated, and freewheeling capitalism.

Now those abiding and ever-true principles of economics have been tainted in the minds of many by recent economic events. As *Newsweek*'s Howard Fineman declared, "The era of cowboy capitalism has died, largely of self-inflicted wounds." So now, those who had been long waiting in the grass to leap up and champion the cause of government-controlled enterprise have made their leap. And for the moment they seem to have landed in a strong and secure position.

We had a taste of this urge for a fierce regulatory revival in late September 2008, when then Democratic Congressman Rahm Emanuel of Illinois (now Obama's chief of staff) warned, in calculated tones of inflamed class resentment, that once the Democrats save the day, they will ensure the end of deregulated markets. (Emanuel, it seems, had previously enjoyed the free market, having worked from 1999 to 2002 at the investment bank Dresdner

Kleinwort Wasserstein in Chicago, where he reportedly earned $18 million.)[3]

I don't believe the free market is doomed, but we definitely have been warned of the coming political pressures. And it is difficult for many supposed conservatives to argue persuasively for pure free-market principles when they have already endorsed the $700 billion bailout and partial nationalization of the credit industry that came down from the Bush administration.

So in the months and years to come, it falls to those of us who advocate for free markets to persist in making our case. It is true that momentary events likely will cloud the public's judgment and provide a nefarious opportunity for liberal statists and other political hustlers. But it is also the truth, which is vouchsafed by any fair reading of history, that excessive regulation and taxation—which means political management of private property and markets—are inherently corrupt and inefficient. Prosperity and the dignity of human freedom are two sides of the same coin. It is an old lesson that now must be re-taught and relearned. And it shall be.

OBAMA'S "HOPES" FOR ECONOMIC "CHANGE"

But for now, we are heading in the opposite direction. President Obama campaigned on a slogan of change. He is supported by overwhelming Democratic majorities in both houses of Congress. And though economic recovery would be accelerated by a perpetuation of the Bush administration's tax cut policy, we're more likely to see the Obama administration do everything wrong with the economy before we can elect someone else to put it right. In the meantime, conservatives in Congress need to be a voice of sanity, reminding voters that the most important step we can take to protect American jobs and keep U.S.-based companies from moving offshore is to reduce sharply our corporate tax rates, which are currently higher than every other major industrial country save economically anemic Japan.

Don't expect that from the Obama administration. Obama's solution to the problem of disappearing jobs and industry is to adopt protectionist policies such as renegotiating NAFTA and opposing new free trade treaties. When one combines Obama's economic protectionism with his plans for environmental regulations to reduce carbon emissions (equivalent to a $100 billion corporate tax hike), his mind-numbingly counterproductive "windfall profit" taxes on oil companies, and his other tax-raising schemes on both business and individuals, one has a formula for economic catastrophe not seen since Herbert Hoover's similar Depression-inducing policies after the stock market crash in 1929.

The fact that Obama has selected a centrist financial team does not mean he is committed to free markets. In fact, he already has assured his base that regardless of who carries out his policies, change will come, "first and foremost," from him personally. On this, I take Obama at his word.

Thomas Babington Macaulay observed that "free trade, one of the greatest blessings which a government can confer on a people, is in almost every country unpopular." The same could be said of high profits and people made rich by free enterprise—without which there cannot be high-paying jobs, sufficient tax revenues for the general welfare and a prosperous society that can afford the arms necessary to defend itself in a violent, covetous world. Though hardly perfect, free markets are the best route for all people, rich and poor alike, to achieve their dreams. To dismantle the free market in the heat of the current moment would surely fulfill Obama's promise of "change." But his other momentous promise—"hope"—would largely be extinguished.

Barack Obama's hostility to the free market is not a position he adopted out of expediency on the campaign trail. Rather, it's a fundamental ideological tenet that anchors his worldview. When he argued in a campaign debate with Hillary Clinton that "fairness" may require him to raise the capital gains tax even if it means less total revenues to the government, he was simply reiterating an idea he has held for many years: that the actual outcome of economic policy—whether it maximizes wealth overall—is not as important as evenly distributing the wealth that exists. In a 2001 radio discussion about the Warren-era Supreme Court, Obama spoke of the overriding importance of achieving this kind of "redistributive justice":

> The Supreme Court never ventured into the issues of redistribution of wealth and more basic issues of political and economic justice in this society. . . . And one of the, I think, the tragedies of the civil rights movement was—because the civil rights movement became so court-focused, I think that there was a tendency to lose track of the political and community organizing and activities on the ground that are able to put together the actual coalitions of power through which you bring about redistributive change.[4]

One must give Obama credit for speaking out so bluntly—that the failure to bring about "redistributive change" was "one of the tragedies of the civil rights movement," and that he, Barack Obama, is committed to putting together "coalitions of power" to achieve that goal.

As the words of an obscure left-wing Illinois state legislator, they are unremarkable. As the political intention of the newly elected president of the United States, while they doubtlessly represent his patriotic hopes for his version of a better America, they present a clear and present danger to the economic system that created the very wealth that Obama is so committed to "redistribute."

President Obama's stated intentions bring to mind Lord Acton's lament regarding the French Revolution: "The finest opportunity ever given to the world was thrown away because the passion for equality made vain the hope for freedom."[5]

This insight applies to our current circumstances as well. The free market may not result in perfect equality, but no system ever has— or ever will. And we hand over control of a growing part of our economic life to the state at our own peril. Throughout American history, we have typically expanded state power during wars or other national security emergencies, then reasserted our personal freedoms once the danger has passed. However, as we saw with the New Deal, when we invite the state to swallow up some part of our economic freedom, we tend not to get it back.

A PROGRAM FOR THE LOYAL OPPOSITION

It is possible that as I write during the bleak final weeks of 2008, I exaggerate in my mind and my words what I see as the coming threat to America's historic freedoms and strength. My side lost an election. It happens to about half the country every four years. Perhaps this is just another passing moment of disappointment. But I think not.

Barack Obama holds out little hope for presiding over a nationalist presidency that would restore America's economic and military strength. What we need in these dangerous times are policies that will reinvigorate the free market, see us through to victory in the war against Islamic terrorism, and cement national unity. But Obama's agenda will accomplish none of that.

America needs a president who is willing to set aside ideological dogmas and put the best interests of America first. Obama remorselessly talked of bipartisanship during the election, but his thin record shows little or no willingness to contradict the favored policies of powerful liberal lobbies. What's more, his past associations with the most virulent anti-American radicals, from the malcontent Reverend Wright to the domestic terrorist Bill Ayers, raise legitimate questions about Obama's deepest views concerning the history, culture, and values of the country he now leads.

One hopes that President Obama will rise to the occasion and become an unapologetic defender of American interests abroad and free markets at home. In such an event, he will deserve our full support. But if he follows through with his campaign promises, then nationalists and conservatives have to be ready to put forward a broad alternative that rejects military weakness and environmental superstition in favor of martial strength, nationalist pride, and economic freedom. The remainder of this book will make the case for such a program, arguing for the policies we must adopt—a military draft, energy independence, wartime measures regarding the law and civil liberties, a truly nationalist foreign policy, a global communications strategy, and a reformed education curriculum—if our great grandchildren a hundred years from now are to look out onto a world, as we still can, from an America still strong enough to guarantee our prosperity, our sovereignty, and our individual freedom.[6]

CHAPTER 2

★　★　★

BRING BACK THE DRAFT

IF THERE'S ONE ISSUE ON WHICH LIBERALS AND CONSERVATIVES AGREE, this is it: they both oppose the draft. To liberals, the draft makes kids cannon-fodder. To conservatives, haunted by memories of the 1960s anti-war movement, it is a surefire prescription for domestic political strife. And libertarians in both camps oppose the draft as a form of involuntary servitude.

Reviving the draft is considered beyond the pale in American politics. The only prominent politician in favor of a draft is New York Democratic congressman Charles Rangel, and he favors it not because of its military utility, but because he wants to embarrass Republicans and make a political statement against the Iraq War.[1] Meanwhile, on the campaign trail Barack Obama acknowledged our dangerous shortfall in military recruiting but proposed no effective remedy; his program for national service—focused on environmentalism instead of the military—will do nothing to replenish our perilously over-stretched armed forces.

But the fact is, the United States needs a bigger army, and we need an army that truly represents the American people. If eternal vigilance is the price of liberty, it is a price that should be paid by all—and that requires national service. A military draft is well within the American tradition, and the scars of the Vietnam-era draft should not keep us from doing what our national interest requires.

For most of the twentieth century, the draft was indispensable for keeping our military strong and cementing national unity. It was par for the course for our fathers and grandfathers. But now, it's considered too politically costly to even discuss. In this environment, very few people bother to consider the entire history of the draft in America, or what a revived draft could contribute to our present war against Islamic extremists and to our overall national security.

I must clarify at the outset that immediately reimposing the draft, of course, is politically unfeasible. The draft will only be adopted when we've formed a national consensus that supports it. More than that, it is not something any president can enact with the stroke of a pen; it requires the approval of Congress, which has the constitutional responsibility for raising and supporting armies. But if we can surmount the emotionalism that infuses this issue and look at the cold, hard facts, I believe many people will reach the same conclusion as I have—that the draft is essential for achieving victory in the long war on Islamist fascism and assuring our capacity to meet the many other threats that are likely to emerge in this already dangerous twenty-first century.

A NOBLE TRADITION

General George Washington advocated conscription during the Revolutionary War, and some states employed it to fill the ranks of their militias. When Washington became president he signed Congress's second Militia Act (1792), calling for all able-bodied white male citizens between the ages of 18 and 45 to be conscripted into their respective state militias. So much for the argument that a military draft contradicts the founding principles of the Republic.

The first federal military draft was signed into law during the Civil War. It had many exemptions, and in the end, fewer than 4 percent of Union troops were draftees. But the very ease of avoiding the draft sparked great resentment against it; many people thought it was unfair, especially because for $300 you could buy your way out of it, or you could find someone to take your place. Although there were initially riots against the draft in New York and elsewhere, such unrest faded once people realized that there were so many exemptions to the draft that it was, in fact, pretty easy to avoid it.[2]

What the draft really accomplished was to encourage the rates of volunteers. As one scholar has pointed out, "The fact that only 3.67 percent of the troops were federal conscripts does not fully reveal the extent to which the draft sustained the Union army.... [I]t stimulated—some might say forced—communities to fill quotas when patriotism began to wane in the last two years of the war. Further, it encouraged another 118,010 Union men to furnish substitutes. When these men are added to the number of conscripts, the federal draft was directly responsible for 13.02 percent of the troops raised from March 1863 through April 1865."[3]

Conscription was abolished after the Civil War, but it was resumed in 1917 when the United States prepared to enter World War I. At the time, the War College Division outlined the weaknesses of the all-volunteer army: "It cannot under the most favorable circumstances produce anything like the number of men required for the national defense. It is undemocratic, unreliable, inefficient and extravagant." The new draft was run through local draft boards staffed by civilians, a reform that greatly increased the fairness of the draft in the eyes of the public.[4]

According to military historian Edward Coffman, the draft met with the "overwhelming acceptance of the public" and "worked very well." There were few instances of organized resistance—mostly by American Indians—and a mere 3,989 men insisted on conscientious objector status. The local draft boards proved incredibly effective, registering 24 million men and supplying the armed forces with a total of 2,758,542 recruits. In fact, the boards were so successful that they provided more men than the army could handle. [5]

The draft was abolished after World War I, only to be revived in 1940 when the United States faced the prospect of entering another world war. The renewed draft, once again run by local draft boards, met with overwhelming public approval. Conscription laws rarely had to be enforced against recalcitrant citizens—the system worked largely through peer pressure, as even reluctant conscripts were unwilling to endure the scorn heaped on those who evaded their military duty.[6]

The key to the draft's popularity during World War II was that it was seen to be fair. "Selective service" was, as its name implied, selective, with certain exemptions—including exemptions for married men, farmers, and workers in war-related industries—but the government promoted the idea that the draft was egalitarian. And when the public saw it being applied to famous actors, professional athletes, and other celebrities, they knew that it was.[7] Public approval of the fairness of local draft boards never fell below 75 percent, and the Gallup polling company observed that "few programs in the nation's history have ever received such widespread favorable reaction from the people as the handling of the Selective Service draft."[8] Most important, the draft once again proved incredibly effective, efficiently mobilizing 11 million men over the course of the war.

Of all the military services, the army relied most heavily on draftees; by 1945, the draft had produced 7 million of the army's 8,300,000 men. As a result, much more than the other services, the army genuinely reflected the American nation. As Lee Kennett notes, if "the other services were to a degree 'hand-picked' from the nation at large, then the Army was the nation itself, an authentic slice of American society with all its many layers. Given the amount of manpower mobilized, it was probably necessary that the Army be that way; given the principles for which the nation fought, it was also somehow appropriate."[9]

The draft expired in 1947, but was revived the following year at the request of President Truman. Conscription was a constant in American life from the beginning of the Cold War to 1973, when it was abolished by President Nixon. It was controversial only toward the end of that period, during the Vietnam War. But in the Korean War, the draft provided half the troops our military needed, and throughout the draft's existence it gave our armed services not just a representative cross-section of the American people, but men with a wide range of needed skills. Military service was a unifying factor for Americans that helped keep our country strong and safe.

IT DOESN'T HAVE TO BE LIKE VIETNAM

But of course during the Vietnam War the draft became not a symbol of unity but of division. The reason was simple: the draft became unpopular because the war became unpopular. In the mid-1960s, when Congress approved the Gulf of Tonkin resolution and President Johnson doubled the number of draft calls, the public still overwhelmingly supported our engagement in Vietnam. Opinion polls showed wide support for our fight against communist expansion into South Vietnam, which was seen as a natural element of our well-established strategy of containment. But rising casualties, an apparent lack of progress in winning the war, an increasingly anti-war media, and the turmoil caused on college campuses and elsewhere by anti-war radicals all eroded support for the war. We should not forget, however, that while anti-war protests sometimes included draft card burnings, the draft was a peripheral issue compared to opposition to the war. As draft historian George Flynn notes,

> When draft resisters were interviewed, some 88 percent justified their action as opposition to the war in Vietnam. Only a little over half were protesting the nature of the draft system itself. This was mainly because very few resisters understood the nature of the draft system. First, a resister identified with an ideology which questioned imperialism, the cold war, social justice at home, the campaign in Vietnam. Only incidentally did he focus on the operation of the draft. To them the draft system was only a symptom of deeper problems.... A lawyer who specialized in defending draft resisters wrote, "I have never yet found one that did not have, at the very nub of his feelings, his opposition to the war." It was "the" war in Vietnam, and not all wars which drew opposition.[10]

This is confirmed even by leftist historians of the Vietnam era. In the introduction to his book on draft "resisters," Michael Foley argues that "draft resistance has been virtually forgotten or, at best, understated by historians of the antiwar movement, the 1960s, and the New Left." He points out that an influential book, Terry Anderson's *The Movement and the Sixties*, devotes just two of its 423 pages to draft resistance, and that even *The Sixties,* a political memoir of the New Left by one of the movement's top radicals, Todd Gitlin, minimizes the impact of anti-draft protests.[11] The reason why the draft receives so little attention, even from leaders of the New Left themselves, is quite clear: the draft was, at best, a minor issue for the movement, which focused almost all its energy on ending the Vietnam War.

Undoubtedly, the Vietnam-era draft was unfair—it granted liberal deferments, especially for college students, which meant that a disproportionate number of draftees came from the lower classes. Yet, the young, working class men who were most likely to be inducted were also among the least likely to oppose the draft. They fulfilled what they regarded as their duty to their country. Instead, what opposition there was came primarily from college students who were exempt from the draft.

So what does Vietnam teach us about the draft? Namely, that conscription will be unpopular during an unpopular war. But the draft should not be viewed as an instrument to force citizens to fight an unpopular war. As was the case during both world wars, the draft is effective at marshalling needed manpower to fight wars that society, by general consensus, deems just and necessary. It also helps to stimulate volunteers who might need that extra incentive to step up and answer the call to duty. After the September 11 terrorist attack, President Bush told us to go shopping to buttress our economy. He might have been better served had he issued a call to Congress and the American people for a new draft to defend our threatened country.

It's natural that we tend to emphasize rights over responsibilities. But in times of national peril, as we will likely face for many years due to the threat of Islamic terrorism, citizens must step forward and accept our obligations to ensure the freedom and safety of our country. America today remains free thanks to the sacrifice of past generations of soldiers, many of whom were conscripts. They understood that our freedom will not endure without an engaged citizenry that is willing, when necessary, to place the needs of the nation above their own.

FACE IT: WE NEED IT

The primary reason for reinstituting the draft is this: our military needs it. When Donald Rumsfeld became Secretary of Defense in 2001, he sought to convert the military into a leaner, meaner, more high-tech fighting force. He took over a military that had already been slashed by the so-called "peace dividend." Between 1990 and 2000, the Army shrank by a quarter of a million troops. The Navy, the Air Force, and the Marine Corps had their manpower reduced by 36 percent, 34 percent, and 12 percent, respectively. National defense spending fell from 5.2 percent of GDP to 3 percent.[12]

To be honest, our military was too small even during the limited conflicts of the 1990s. But Rumsfeld believed that by relying on high-tech weaponry and special forces, we could do more with less. The initial success of the invasion of Afghanistan seemed to prove him right, as did the early triumphs in Iraq. But when it quickly became apparent—as it had always been to some generals, and as it was to a handful of politicians, most famously Senator John McCain—that more forces were needed, our leaders were reluctant to respond because we did not have a large reserve of troops to throw into the battle.

But imagine how the situation in Iraq would have developed if, after our lean, elite forces had overthrown Saddam's army and regime, they were followed by three or four hundred thousand occupation troops protecting every major building, town, and village. The post-invasion insurgency would have been quickly suppressed—if it broke out at all—and Iraq would have been a political triumph and an object lesson to enemies of the United States.

The bottom line is that despite all our technological advantages, troop strength matters. Even the addition of just 20,000 to 30,000 troops in Iraq during the "surge"—announced in January 2007, nearly four years after the start of the war—completely changed the complexion of the conflict. Before the surge, U.S. forces repeatedly swept areas of terrorists, but because we lacked the manpower to hold our secure areas the terrorists quickly returned. The surge changed that. In March 2007, General Petraeus described the surge's success: "After our guys are in the neighborhood for four or five days, the people realize they're not going to just leave them like we did in the past. Then they begin to come in with so much information on the enemy that we can't process it fast enough."[13] In the second half of 2007, after the surge reached its full force, violence in Iraq declined by 60 percent,[14] forcing even Democratic congressman Jack Murtha, a die-hard opponent of the Iraq War, to admit that the surge was working.[15] In fact, the surge worked so well that Iraq was hardly an issue in the 2008 elections.

The surge's dramatic success proved that in the end there's no substitute for boots on the ground. We need troops to kick in doors, troops to gather intelligence, and troops to assure local civilians that the United States is committed to eradicating terrorists. This is what's needed now to reverse the deteriorating situation in Afghanistan, where General David McKiernan, the commander of NATO forces in Afghanistan, has pleaded for the transfer of four more brigades "as quickly as possible" to bolster undermanned U.S. forces there.[16] McKiernan, however, notes that securing new troops for Afghanistan depends on the situation in Iraq.[17] Thankfully, now that the surge in Iraq has worked, troops may become available to shift to Afghanistan, although the numbers are not enough to meet General McKiernan's requests.[18] It's a shame that our troops in Afghanistan have had to fight shorthanded for so many years because we can't field enough soldiers to accomplish our goals.

The dramatic effect of the surge in Iraq raises an obvious question: why didn't we send more troops sooner? The answer was made clear in a meeting President Bush convened in December 2006 to discuss military strategy in Iraq with the Joint Chiefs of Staff, who opposed a surge strategy. According to the *Washington Post*, "A constant subtext in the meeting yesterday, and in the ongoing White House review, is the Joint Chiefs' growing concern about the erosion of the U.S. military's ability to deal with other crises around the world because of the heavy commitment in Iraq and the stress on troops and equipment, said officials familiar with the review. The chiefs planned to tell Bush of the significantly increased risk to readiness in the event of a new emergency, rather than push for a timeline to leave Iraq."[19]

It should worry us all that the addition of just 20,000–30,000 badly needed troops in Iraq meant, the Joint Chiefs feared, that we might be unable to handle another military crisis. No superpower can afford to be so short-handed; no superpower can afford that sort of vulnerability. In November 2007 Army Chief of Staff General George Casey told the Senate Armed Services Committee, "We are consumed with meeting the demands for the current fight and unable to provide ready forces as rapidly as necessary for other contingencies." In fact, the lack of available ground troops has led some officials and analysts to conclude that if the United States found another unavoidable military conflict, we would have to rely on air power and even, if it was serious enough, nuclear weapons.[20] Our shortfall of troops deprives our commander in chief of the sort of flexible military response he should have.

To find more troops, the army has boosted pay, increased the frequency of bonuses, begun paying recruits' graduate school tuition, increased the use of waivers for recruits with criminal records, and raised the maximum age for new recruits to forty-two. Yet General William S. Wallace, the commander of Army Training and Doctrine Command, reported that the Army began its 2007 recruiting year (beginning October 1, 2007) with fewer people registered for basic training than in any year since the end of the draft in 1973.[21]

The army's manpower crisis is exacerbated by severe problems in officer retention, which has fallen to its lowest rate in decades. The attrition rate of junior officers with between four and nine years of experience jumped from approximately 8 percent in 2003 to 13 percent in 2006. By 2007 the army faced a shortage of 3,000 captains and majors, with that shortfall expected to double by 2010. What's more, the army is losing its brightest, most capable officers, with internal army memos warning of the "disproportionate loss of high-potential, high-performance junior leaders."

The exodus of officers from the army is a major problem that looks to grow even worse. According to the *Wall Street Journal*, there is "mounting evidence that the long wars are pushing many young officers out of the Army. The number of West Point graduates leaving the military as soon as their initial tours are up is at a 25-year high. Nearly half of the academy's class of 2001 left active duty in 2006, compared with a normal five-year dropout rate of 10% to 30%, according to Cindy Williams, a military-manpower expert at the Massachusetts Institute of Technology."[22]

Even if the all-volunteer force could find a way to attract more recruits, it's an open question, as Andrew Tilghman notes,

Who is going to lead these new forces if seasoned young officers continue leaving the Army in droves? Calls to expand the Army are empty rhetoric if the military brass and their civilian bosses fail to grapple with whether the services can recruit and retain junior leaders in both numbers and quality. The Army has struggled to meet the increase of 30,000 troops authorized since 2004. This year, new laws call for an additional increase of 65,000 during the next five years. But according to the Congressional Budget Office, if recruiting and retention does not improve from 2005 levels, the Army's end strength will actually decline.[23]

The shortfall in recruits is a serious threat to the integrity of the army. This was confirmed by Barry McCaffrey, a retired four-star general now teaching at West Point, who argued after visiting Iraq in 2006 that the war has left our undermanned military "in a position of strategic peril." He also noted that the army has had to lower recruiting standards, leading to the entry of increasing numbers of drug abusers, high school drop-outs, and convicted criminals into the army. The undermanned National Guard is experiencing similar recruiting and retention problems, despite rapidly increasing enlistment and re-enlistment bonuses. In fact, McCaffrey warned that the continued mobilization of National Guard brigades for combat tours in Iraq could "topple" the entire National Guard structure.[24]

In October 2007, Lieutenant General Michael Rochelle, deputy chief of staff for personnel, revealed that in order to sustain manpower, 9,000 U.S. soldiers were forced to stay on duty past their retirement or reenlistment dates. This means that the U.S. already has a de facto draft—one that applies only to patriotic Americans who were selfless enough to have volunteered for military duty.

In reality, there is little the military can do to attract more recruits. According to the Congressional Budget Office, enlisted personnel are already paid better than 75 percent of American civilians with similar education levels.[25] The fact is, there is a limit to the number of people willing to volunteer to be a soldier—a dangerous career that is often severely disruptive of family life—and that pool has clearly been tapped out.

The Joint Chiefs were correct in warning President Bush that the surge in Iraq would detract from our ability to address other international crises. While it's unlikely that we'll find ourselves in a land war against a behemoth like the Chinese Army in the near future, we will clearly be involved militarily in Afghanistan, and perhaps Iraq, for years to come, even as other potential flashpoints in Pakistan, Iran, and elsewhere take on an ever growing urgency. The communist threats facing Taiwan and South Korea are unlikely to disappear anytime soon, and we are subject to an increasingly aggressive and anti-Western foreign policy from a resurgent Russia that aims to monopolize Europe's energy supply. And note that the Pentagon recently created a new military command in Africa—AFRICOM—to fight if necessary on the African continent. It's yet another military responsibility added without any new troops to carry out the mission.

Moreover, many experts believe that regional wars over oil and water are increasingly likely, as evidenced by, among other things, China's stationing of Red Army troops to protect their oil sites in Sudan. And if Saudi Arabia's oil fields ever had to be defended from an Iranian attack, we could be forced to garrison troops and fight throughout the Middle Eastern theater.

We will soon be faced with the choice of severely scaling back our role in the world or expanding the army through conscription. I won't say that in principle a conscripted army is superior to an all-volunteer force. To the contrary, I believe an all-volunteer force is preferable; I know many young men and women in the volunteer military—including one of my sons—and they all believe in the quality and esprit de corps of the volunteer military. I also acknowledge that reinstituting the draft will entail many costs, both monetarily and in terms of lost freedom. However, we must face the reality that, given our current international commitments, and the likelihood that these commitments will grow, we will need a bigger army than our current all-volunteer force.

A larger, conscripted army need not resemble the tsarist-era model of peasant cannon fodder. Instead, the army should continue to press all its technological advantages, but it also must ensure that it has enough troops. As defense policy analyst Thomas Donnelly and military historian Frederick Kagan warn, "The limitations of America's land forces remain the most fundamental constraint on U.S. military strategy. Unless we begin now to restore and reshape the services to do what we have asked them to do, there will be tragic consequences: not that our Army and Marine Corps will be 'broken,' but that our nation will not win the war that it is in."[26]

The questions that any statesman or strategist has to confront are obvious: What if our armed forces are suddenly needed to take out Iran's nuclear program? What if Pakistan falls to the jihadists, and we need troops to secure that country's nuclear weapons? What if China invades Taiwan? What if North Korea, in a desperate gambit, launches an attack on South Korea? What if the vast resources of the North Pole spark a military rivalry between Russia, Canada, the United States, and other countries? What if the Saudi oil fields require protection? What if we have to secure our southern border from increasingly ambitious drug cartels or civil disturbances in Mexico?

Unfortunately, it's highly unlikely that President Obama will bring to our military the fighting strength it so desperately needs. Obama acknowledges the need for more troops and vows to add 65,000 troops to the army and 27,000 to the Marines. But he proposes no way of recruiting even these woefully insufficient numbers other than by increasing various military benefits—the same failing strategy we have now. In addressing our end strength problems in his official defense program, aside from allowing openly gay soldiers to serve, Obama simply promises to "inspire today's youth to serve our nation the same way President Kennedy once did," and to "restore the ethic of public service to the agenda."[27] Such meaningless platitudes will do nothing to rejuvenate our deteriorating military; Obama's belief that his inspiring personality will send men and women flooding to enlist tells us more about his self-regard than it does about how he will solve our military manpower crisis.

What's more, it's doubtful whether Obama even understands the fundamental importance of our military. "We cannot continue to rely only on our military in order to achieve the national security objectives that we've set," he argues, adding that "we've got to have a civilian national security force that's just as powerful, just as strong, just as well funded."[28] The notion that Obama can recruit nearly one-and-a-half million people to serve in his ill-defined "national security force," and that he can find more than half a trillion dollars every year to fund it, and that this force will match the power of the U.S. military, is not a proposal that can be taken seriously. Obama clearly has no real plan to expand the military even though, to his credit, he understands that it is necessary. And his insincerity on this fundamental issue does not bode well for our national security under his presidency.

GET WITH THE PROGRAM

The only way to increase significantly the size of our military is the hard way, the proven way, through the draft. This should be instituted as part of a universal program of national service. I recognize that the Democratic Congress is extremely unlikely to take this step, but national service, besides its military utility, would have many other benefits for our country that Democrats might find attractive.

For a party that hails the benefits of "diversity," national service would be a way to take a country as diverse as our own and bring it greater national cohesion and unity. It is undeniable that our society is becoming more atomized, that common cultural reference points are becoming fewer, and that our sense of community is declining. As Professor Robert Putnam, author of *Bowling Alone,* has noted, "The closing decades of the twentieth century found Americans growing ever less connected with one another and with collective life. We voted less, joined less, gave less, trusted less, invested less time in public affairs, and engaged less with our friends, our neighbors, and even our families. Our 'we' steadily shriveled."[29]

I would not claim, of course, that a system of national service would fix all these ills, but it would, undeniably, help. And we will need that help. Technology, for all its benefits, divides people at least as much as it unites them, as it closes people off in their own self-contained electronic worlds. Rising ethnic and cultural diversity, with more Americans speaking different languages at home and practicing different religions, with multiculturalism regnant in our schools—all these factors lessen our sense of common purpose and common destiny. Many citizens increasingly view our country as simply the place where they happen to live, instead of feeling pride in a common history and culture.

While individualism has always been a vital element of our culture, it has metastasized into a fetish that would be unrecognizable by George Washington, Thomas Jefferson, or even Thomas Paine. National service will help return us to the proper balance of citizen duties and rights that guided our nation so well for its first two centuries. It would connect all Americans, men and women, through the shared experience of sacrificing for the greater good of the nation.

If you want a striking example of how America has changed, consider this: after the Japanese attacked pearl Harbor, World War I-era recruiting posters were resurrected with Uncle Sam pointing at every passerby and declaring, "I Want You" to join the army. Tens of thousands of Americans heeded the call and volunteered for the military, and everyone was asked to contribute to the war effort in some way. In contrast, after the September 11, 2001, terrorist attacks, which claimed even more lives than the attack on Pearl Harbor, President George W. Bush encouraged us to live our lives as normal, to go to the mall and shop. Remarkably, President Bush never dedicated a single major speech to urging young Americans to join the military and fight for our country.

But it's not just the former president's failure. As Kathy Roth-Douquet and Frank Schaeffer observed, the *New York Times* and other major newspapers endorsed the invasion of Afghanistan after September 11, but none of them called on Americans to join the military. They note, "Perhaps, though they believed the war was theoretically just, the idea of someone actually fighting it simply made them too uncomfortable."

Or maybe our media and social elites simply don't want their own children to serve. Elite society has become expert at insisting on its rights, but no longer seems interested in shouldering the responsibility of military service. In 1956, 400 out of 750 members of Princeton's graduating class joined the military; in 2004, only nine of them did, which was the most of any Ivy League school.[30]

Many elite campuses now ban ROTC completely, while other schools' administrators and even students do all they can to keep out military recruiters.

It can't be good for our country when the nation's elites opt out of their responsibilities to service, especially military service. I have some personal experience with this anti-military animus; when one of my sons joined the army, his friends and neighbors—all good and decent middle class people—passionately urged him to reconsider. It does not speak well of our sense of common purpose that in a time of war, middle-class Americans think that they're too good to fight it.

Today, we have a dedicated all-volunteer military which, despite all the pressures on it, still enlists, commissions, trains, and promotes many of the best and brightest people we have. But the military culture is increasingly distinct from an American culture that is too-often materialistic and self-absorbed. Unfortunately, self-fulfillment seems to have replaced the idea of obligation; rights have displaced the idea of duty; and shopping has taken the place of service. That is not a model for a successful society, let alone one at war, let alone one facing an existential threat from radical Islam.

Barack Obama campaigned in favor of a national service program, but it's almost entirely divorced from military concerns. Instead, Obama's entire plan is a typical New Deal/New Frontier/Great Society combination of faux idealism and liberal patronage: a make-work program for young people. Obama's program is national service lite, focused on feel-good measures—like sending young Americans overseas "to ensure our voice is heard"—that are designed to achieve little more than giving well-off youths a memorable life experience. Furthermore, with its emphasis on fighting global warming and its advocacy of a "clean energy corps," a "green job corps," and even a "green vet initiative," Obama's program is more geared toward drafting Americans into the environmental movement than actually serving and helping to defend our country.

If I were to devise for Congress a system of national service, it would look something like this: It would be a compulsory program for all Americans aged eighteen or ninteen, men and women, after most have graduated from high school. The military, reviewing these graduates' transcripts, extracurricular activities, and medical reports, would select however many they needed to fulfill their draft allotments for a two-year period of military service. Those not chosen by the military would undertake a two-year civil service obligation.

Those in the latter category could be used in auxiliary roles to assist in homeland security. Using civil recruits in clerical, technical, and other capacities for the police, border patrol, and other law enforcement agencies would free up needed manpower for patrols. They could also inspect cargo at our nation's ports, which remain a crucial weak point of our homeland security efforts.[31]

Aside from homeland security functions, civil recruits could be trained to meet other crucial shortages in service occupations. A good example is nursing home attendants. With the aging of the baby boom generation, we can expect a rapid expansion in the number of nursing home residents in the coming years. Many nursing homes are already turning to illegal immigrants to staff their facilities, but wouldn't it be better for elderly Americans to be cared for by young Americans?

Civil recruits could contribute in many other ways to improving America. They could assist in understaffed schools, help build homes for the poor, or train in local disaster relief. The entire program could be operated along the lines of Americorps, which sends members to work with established non-profit, public service, faith-based, and community organizations. That way recruits will be assigned to work on real community needs, rather than bureaucratic "make-work" projects.

The crucial point would be that every American would be obliged to spend two years working to make our country safer and better, even at the cost of personal sacrifice. National service would take every young American—of all races and religions, classes and types, the idealists and the couch potatoes—and give them a sense of what it means to be a member of this country, to truly understand the obligations as well as the rights of citizenship.

SERVICE NOT SERVITUDE

Naturally, libertarians, such as I once was, will instinctively reject this entire proposal as "involuntary servitude." But William F. Buckley Jr., who had no shortage of libertarian instincts himself, rejected the libertarian argument and supported the idea of national service (even laying out his own plan in his book, *Gratitude*). As Buckley wrote, conservatives rightly perceive "connections between the individual and the community beyond those that relate either to the state or to the marketplace." The free market is vital to America's well-being, but without an animating national spirit underlying it, our country will degenerate into nothing more than a giant trading bazaar where many different people happen to live together. While national service is necessarily directed by the state, its purpose, especially in the civil component (Buckley's plan did not have a military component) is directed specifically at strengthening our sense of community.

Moreover, the libertarian argument collapses in the face of history. Our Founding Fathers fervently supported the idea that government has the right, and indeed the duty, to instill patriotic and

moral values. Buckley quotes from the Senate's reply to George
Washington's First Inaugural Address:

> We feel, Sir, the force and acknowledge the justness of the
> observation, that the foundation of our national policy
> should be laid in private morality. If individuals be not influ-
> enced by moral principles, it is in vain to look for public
> virtue; it is, therefore, the duty of legislators to enforce, both
> by precept and example, the utility as well as the necessity,
> of a strict adherence to the rules of distributive justice.

The founders never shied away from inculcating in Americans a
sense of patriotism, civic duty, and morality. And they would certainly do so now, because, as Buckley noted, we live in "a society
that seems not to be effectively transmitting, to our successor citizens, those ideas we cling to as indispensable to the characterization
of a proud society."

National service is a call to renew the self-sacrifice, patriotism,
and stoicism that once animated our country, but that today seem
too often shelved in favor of a self-centered veneration of personal
happiness. I grant you that national service would be a costly
endeavor, and would undoubtedly provoke libertarian outrage from
a number of eighteen-year-olds who've become estranged from the
very idea of a citizen's obligation to his country. But the question is
this: is enlarging America's military to defend our vital national
interests and renew our sense of national unity worth the price of a
national service program? I think the answer is undeniably yes.
More than that, I believe it's inevitable, if we are to survive and
prosper as a free and independent nation.[32]

★ ★ ★

CHAPTER 3

AMERICA HELD HOSTAGE

O UR NATIONAL SECURITY IS BEING HELD HOSTAGE BY OUR RELIANCE on foreign oil. We need a nationalist energy policy, one that secures the energy we need, at a cost we can afford, and ensures our independence. That sounds like a tall order—but it shouldn't be. America's current energy woes are the direct result of political failure, of the failure of our government to have the foresight and determination to achieve what should be obvious goals—goals that have been clear at least since the 1973 OPEC oil boycott.

Simply put, America needs oil. We currently import around 66 percent of our crude oil, of which around 20 percent comes from the Persian Gulf. We have three carrier groups in the Gulf to guarantee the free flow of 17 million barrels of oil through the Strait of Hormuz every day. As the International Energy Agency's Lawrence Eagles observed, the possibility of a hostile power (like Iran) blocking the strait "is probably the biggest single energy security risk that exists in the world."[1]

A severe disruption of our oil supply, as we saw in 1973, would cause extensive economic dislocation in America and abroad. Securing a steady supply of energy is a vital national interest. Even the American left, on some level, understands this—notwithstanding the "no blood for oil" cant favored by many liberals, they know full well that a full-blown energy crisis would severely harm U.S. industry, leaving a lot less tax money for social programs. President Carter may have responded to an energy crunch by turning down the heat and donning a cozy sweater, but no administration will last long that tries to make Americans do the same. After one term in office, Carter found that out for himself.

Our reliance on Middle Eastern oil is a strategic liability that has already forced us into at least one war: the first Gulf War, when we sent hundreds of thousands of troops to the Gulf to liberate Kuwait and defend Saudi Arabia from Saddam Hussein. But even while acting as the Gulf States' protector, we have surprisingly little political clout over these countries because of our dependence on their black gold.

Take Qatar. It's only defense against being annexed by Iran is the United States military. And yet, Qatar is home to the hugely influential, anti-American, pro-jihadist "news" network al-Jazeera. The network, which specializes in broadcasting al Qaeda propaganda tapes, including those made by Osama bin Laden himself, was created and is subsidized by our supposed ally, the Emir of Qatar.

Even more damaging is our acquiescence to the Saudis' massive program to spread Wahhabi Islam, a virulently anti-Western, anti-Christian, and anti-Jewish ideology linked to that of Osama bin Laden and the suicide killers who struck on September 11, 2001. The Saudis have invested billions of dollars of their oil wealth in spreading this ideology all over the world through a large network of Saudi-funded schools and "charitable" and cultural organizations. Among their "successes" was educating the Taliban in Afghanistan, the hosts of Osama bin Laden and al Qaeda.

The Saudis' Wahhabi propaganda program has especially targeted Central Asia, Russia, and Bosnia. But it also extends to America itself, particularly through a campaign to build mosques and staff them with Saudi-vetted Wahhabi imams. A 2006 Freedom House investigation found that anti-Christian and anti-Semitic hate literature funded by the Saudi government was rife in American mosques. The report warned that the fact that this incitement was "being mainstreamed within our borders through the efforts of a foreign government, namely Saudi Arabia, demands our urgent attention."[2]

Yet, has the outrageous problem of Saudi incitement against Christians and Jews within America's own borders received any meaningful attention in Washington? When was the last time you read an article about any government initiative to combat this phenomenon? The truth of the matter is that our leverage with the Saudis is limited by our dependence on their oil. In order to guarantee access to that oil, we are committed to defending the Saudi kingdom, as we did in the Gulf War. And yet, even as the Saudi sheiks bask content in our military protection, they act as the chief ideological sponsors of worldwide Islamic radicalism.

By breaking our dependence on Middle Eastern oil, we would break the chains that bind us to Saudi Arabia and the Gulf States and establish a new source of American influence. Although world oil prices have declined steeply from the dizzying levels reached in mid-2008, rising demand for energy in China, India, and other developing nations, alongside sharply falling production from the world's existing oil fields,[3] means that the days of cheap oil are numbered—and when our economy picks up, we will add mightily to world oil demand. The huge income flows generated from oil and other natural resources guarantee that energy-rich states will become even more powerful in the future than they are now, while energy importers will fall increasingly under the sway of their suppliers. The good news is that the United States is well-endowed with energy resources, if Congress will allow us to tap them. And it better, because other countries are looking to squeeze America and American interests in an energy vice.

While the war on Islamic terrorists receives the biggest headlines these days, countries are waging a constant struggle over the world's energy resources. If current trends continue, competition for these resources will become even more intense. Tensions over resource-rich areas, both on land and offshore, will result in an explosion of what has been called "resource wars."[4] There is only one way America can avoid getting drawn into these kinds of conflicts: by developing our own natural resources and breaking our energy dependence on foreign countries. If America fails to achieve this goal, the twenty-first century will be a much bloodier one for us than it need be.

OIL AS A WEAPON

Governments that use their natural resources to expand their international power are nothing new. But the explosion in energy prices over the last decade has provided an irresistible temptation for many governments to become more directly involved in energy production. When a strongman leader sees an opportunity to enhance his domestic popularity with oil-funded social programs and simultaneously gain leverage over oil-importing countries, it's rare that he'll look the other way.

Take Venezuela, where neo-socialist Hugo Chavez is using Venezuelan oil wealth to spread his brand of socialist revolution within his own country and abroad. Venezuela's oil revenues have allowed Chavez to create a system of socialized medicine, large-scale public works projects, state-funded "workers' cooperatives," and a rapidly expanding military, not to mention a burgeoning state-sponsored personality cult. Chavez has established personal control over the Venezuelan state oil company, Petroleos de Venezuela (PDVSA), by firing its management along with thousands of politically unreliable workers and replacing them with his own loyalists. He also nationalized four giant oil ventures, pushing foreign oil companies out of the projects or forcing them to cede majority control to PDVSA.

The result has been a cash bonanza for the Venezuelan government. But Chavez has dedicated this bounty to a greater purpose than merely buying the support of his own people. He has systematically used Venezuela's oil fortunes as a tool of foreign policy. And he's been quite open about what country his policies are aimed against, proclaiming that Venezuela has "a strong oil card to play on the geopolitical stage.... It is a card that we are going to play with toughness against the toughest country in the world, the United States."[5]

Although Chavez has not yet followed through on his periodic threats to reduce or ban oil sales to America, which consumes 60 percent of Venezuela's oil exports,[6] he has increased cooperation with American rivals such as China, Iran, Cuba, and Russia in hopes of increasing his leverage over the United States. He has pushed within OPEC to cut production levels in order to drive up oil prices and squeeze American consumers, and he has used Venezuela's oil-backed diplomatic power to establish Mercosur, a Latin American trading bloc, as a bastion of opposition to U.S.

influence in Latin America. He's also committed to spending billions of dollars to strengthen the Venezuelan military to fight off what he has repeatedly claimed to be an imminent American invasion.[7]

Chavez will continue to gain leverage over America so long as we keep importing more than a million barrels of oil a month from him, making Venezuela one of the top four U.S. oil suppliers. This leverage shows itself in part in his ability to alienate Latin American countries from the United States.

His populist policies have spawned a number of homegrown Chavez clones in other Latin American nations, most notably in Bolivia, where fellow socialist Evo Morales was elected president in 2005 after running on an anti-American, pro-Chavez platform. Working off Chavez's example, Morales nationalized Bolivia's natural gas reserves, forcing all foreign gas companies in Bolivia to sell majority stakes in their Bolivian holdings to the Bolivian government. Like Chavez, Morales has shown little regard for democratic niceties, sending in government goon squads to attack protesting workers and calling a rigged constitutional assembly in order to increase presidential powers and codify socialist policies in Bolivia's constitution.

Although such policies have made Morales increasingly unpopular at home and have even spawned a growing separatist movement in Bolivia's eastern oil and gas producing regions, Morales' position is strengthened by Chavez, who has reached into his country's oil wealth to launch a massive foreign aid program for Bolivia. As a Bolivian opposition senator ruefully noted, "We've become a client state of Venezuela, in what is a new form of imperialism."[8]

Venezuela has developed a similar authority over communist Cuba, which has become virtually a ward of Venezuela. Chavez supplies Cuba's communist regime with 100,000 barrels of discounted oil a year, which equates to a $2 billion annual subsidy, a crucial source of support for Cuba's failed economy.[9] Unsurprisingly, with their leaders utterly dependent on Chavez's oil wealth, Bolivia and Cuba have joined a tripartite coalition with Venezuela, directed against the United States.

Venezuela's oil money also helped fund—or was meant to help fund—the election of Argentina's leftwing president Cristina Fernandez de Kirchner. In August 2007, while Kirchner was running for president, Argentinean officials nabbed a Venezuelan businessman with a suitcase stuffed with nearly $800,000 in undeclared cash. The businessman, Guido Antonini Wilson, had arrived in Argentina on a flight from Venezuela along with several Argentinean government officials and executives from PDVSA, the Venezuelan state oil company. The money, Wilson later admitted, was intended as an illegal campaign contribution to Kirchner from the Venezuelan government. In November 2008 Venezuelan Franklin Duran was convicted in the United States of acting as an illegal foreign agent for his efforts to silence Wilson and to cover up the entire episode on behalf of the Venezuelan government. Duran was the fourth man convicted in the case.

Chavez also inserted himself into elections in Nicaragua, signing an agreement with members of the leftist opposition to sell cheap oil to Nicaragua in order to boost the electoral fortunes of "former" communist and anti-American stalwart Daniel Ortega, who was duly elected president in November 2006. [10]

Around the same time, Chavez backed Raphael Correa's successful bid for the presidency of Ecuador. Correa, who had been forced to resign as Ecuadoran finance minister after secretly arranging a $300 million loan from Chavez, ran a campaign featuring Chavez-like rhetoric attacking international oil companies and vowing to rewrite the constitution to strengthen socialism. A bitter critic of the United States, he also denounced a proposed U.S.–Ecuadoran free trade deal, advocated closing a U.S. military base in Ecuador, and heaped personal insults on President Bush. Correa's opponent in the election repeatedly accused Chavez of funding Correa's campaign, although Correa denied the charge.

Correa also denied rumors that he maintained close relations with FARC, a narco-terrorist group responsible for an untold number of killings and kidnappings in Colombia, a U.S. ally. Correa's denials, however, wore thin in March 2008, when Colombia raided a FARC base in Ecuador and killed Raul Reyes, a senior FARC commander. Colombia accused Correa of giving sanctuary to FARC, and reported that a laptop computer seized in the raid showed that FARC received direct funding from Chavez. Denouncing Colombian president Alvaro Uribe as a U.S. puppet, Chavez responded to the raid by threatening war against Colombia and moving Venezuelan troops to the Colombian border.[11]

On the international stage Chavez is a buffoon, but we can't simply dismiss him, because his oil wealth elevates him to the level of an international menace, a reviver of communism and terrorism in Latin America. And we, unfortunately, are the world's biggest buyer of Venezuelan oil exports.

ENERGY IN RUSSIA: PUTTING THE SQUEEZE ON OUR ALLIES

Saudi Arabia and Venezuela are not the only countries that have transformed their domestic oil supply into a potent geopolitical weapon. The same strategy is evident in Russia, the world's second largest oil producer and its number one natural gas producer. After initially governing as a relatively pro-market reformer, in 2003 former Russian president Vladimir Putin moved against Yukos, a top Russian oil producer with a reputation as one of the country's most well-managed private corporations. Prosecutors had the company's president, Mikhail Khodorkhovsky, sentenced to eight years in jail on tax evasion charges, and they filed a series of multi-billion dollar tax evasion claims against Yukos. These claims were used as a pretext for the government to break up the firm and sell off its core production unit to a state-owned company, Rosneft, through a rigged auction. Likewise, under Putin's presidency, the Russian state assumed control of Sibneft, another major oil producer, and has regained a controlling position in Gazprom, a corporate giant that is the world's largest natural gas producer as well as Russia's monopoly gas exporter.

In order to further consolidate state control of Russia's energy supply, Putin leaned on western energy companies operating in Russia. Authorities forced British Petroleum's Russian subsidiary to sell off its majority stake in a major natural gas project in the Kovykta fields to Gazprom, while they pressured a consortium of Shell, Mitsubishi, and Mitsui into ceding majority control to Gazprom of a lucrative gas project in Sakhalin for a cut-rate price.

Many analysts interpreted Putin's initial moves against Yukos as an isolated event designed to punish Khodorkovsky for his plans to run against Putin for the presidency. However, as Putin continued to consolidate Russia's energy supply in state hands, it became clear that the state takeover of Yukos was part of a wider campaign to bolster Russia's international influence by reasserting state dominance over Russia's vast energy resources.

From the beginning of his presidency, Putin, who has bemoaned the downfall of the Soviet Union as "the greatest geopolitical catastrophe of the century," sought to restore the international power wielded by Russia's former communist regime. Initially, this seemed a herculean task. When Putin became president in 2000, Russia was in chaos. The country was an economic mess, and the Red Army had atrophied into a superannuated force that could not even defeat Islamic separatists in the Russian Republic of Chechnya. But Putin is a highly intelligent, politically savvy leader with a deep understanding of power. Early in his presidency, he realized that the route to re-establishing Russian influence was not through the traditional Russian method of fielding a massive army, but rather through a different route—through energy.

Having seized control of Yukos and other key domestic energy companies, the Putin government reaped a windfall from the spike in oil and natural gas prices that lasted throughout Putin's presidency. Standing outside of OPEC, Russia has an especially envious position in the world oil market, since it benefits from higher oil prices when OPEC cuts production, while remaining free to set its own production levels. With the giant profits from state-controlled energy production, Putin balanced Russia's federal budget (which has run a surplus since 2001), paid off the country's Soviet-era debt to international creditors, and created a "stabilization fund" in 2004 that is now split between a $30 billion "national welfare fund," which operates like a sovereign wealth fund, and a "reserve fund" worth an incredible $140 billion.

The national welfare fund, which is expected soon to begin investing in foreign companies, could become another powerful lever of Russian state influence. As the *Moscow Times* noted in 2008, "While the amount held by Russia's sovereign wealth fund is relatively small, it is growing rapidly. Finance Minister Alexei Kudrin told the recent World Economic Forum in Davos that windfall profits would surpass $200 billion this year. This is a significant amount of cash—enough to acquire significant stakes in foreign companies or to meddle with another country's currency market."[12]

Although the current economic crisis has severely depressed the Russian stock market and limited the growth of Russia's national welfare and reserve funds, Russian leaders have indicated they view this as a great opportunity to buy up cheap Western assets; in the words of Putin, "Perhaps we should buy something [abroad]? Something that is up for grabs?"[13]

Of course, thanks to their near-limitless oil wealth, Abu Dhabi, Kuwait, Saudi Arabia, and other countries have created their own sovereign wealth funds that actively invest in American companies. Although the managers of these funds inevitably claim that they only seek to maximize profits, these protestations are not credible; since these are state-run enterprises, their ultimate goal is to further their governments' national interests. And the national interest of a country like Saudi Arabia is emblazoned on its flag for all to see— to spread the belief that "There is no God but Allah, and Mohammed is his prophet."

Likewise, Putin is using Russia's energy riches to pursue national goals, having parlayed state-controlled energy companies into a formidable source of international power. This was evident during Russia's 2005–2006 gas dispute with Ukraine. Shortly after the election in Ukraine of pro-Western president Viktor Yushchenko, who had vowed to move Ukraine away from Russia's sphere of influence, Gazprom decided to raise prices on its natural gas exports to Ukraine to market levels. These prices, which had been heavily subsidized since the Soviet days, were slated to increase by several hundred percent. After Ukraine balked at Gazprom's demands, the company on January 1, 2006, cut off Ukraine's gas supply. Faced with a lack of gas for heating homes in the middle of winter, Ukraine apparently siphoned off gas from Gazprom's transit pipelines that move gas from Russia through Ukraine to Eastern and Western Europe, resulting in serious gas shortages throughout much of the continent. Amidst howls of protest from European leaders, Ukraine and Gazprom quickly agreed on a new price scheme, and after three days Gazprom resumed Ukraine's gas supply. European politicians belatedly recognized how vulnerable they had become to energy blackmail by Russia, which accounts for roughly a quarter of the EU's oil and natural gas supplies, but, typically, they did nothing about it.

Indeed, Western Europe will more likely submit to Russian energy blackmail than do something to contest it. When Russia invaded Georgia in August 2008, European protests against Russian aggression were noticeably muted, especially from the bigger importers of Russian energy, like Germany. Any statesman looking to the future would assume that Russian energy dominance over the continent is going to grow.

Not content with reasserting state control of much of its own energy supply, Russia has aggressively sought to expand its ownership of European pipelines and energy companies. Gazprom has been particularly successful in this regard, demanding and receiving stakes in various countries' energy companies as part of negotiations over the price of its natural gas supplies. In order to counter Russia's growing energy dominance, the United States, and to a lesser extent the European Union, have attempted to secure gas supplies that do not originate in or transit through Russia. This has touched off a new version of the nineteenth century great game in Central Asia, as America seeks the cooperation of the region's energy producers to build pipelines that bypass Russia, while the Kremlin seeks to lock those nations into mutual supply and transit agreements.

Russia has gained the clear upper hand in this contest, as the U.S.-proposed pipelines have mostly come to naught; in May 2007, a major agreement was reached to restore and expand a pipeline to move gas from Turkmenistan through Kazakhstan into Russia, thus thwarting U.S. hopes for a non-Russian route across the Caspian Sea. Meanwhile, Europe has failed in its feeble attempts to diversify its energy supplies away from Russia. To the contrary, construction is currently underway on Nord Stream, a new pipeline to send gas under the Baltic Sea from Russia directly to Germany. " 'I think you can now say that Russia has either won the war or is very close to winning the war over gas supplies,' said Chris Weafer, chief strategist at UralSib, a Russian investment bank. 'Because the EU, which sought non-Russian import routes and non-Russian gas supplies, has failed to achieve anything.'"[14]

What's more, the EU is set to become even more susceptible to energy blackmail now that Russia, Iran, and Qatar have begun discussions to establish an OPEC-like cartel for natural gas. As Europe becomes ever more dependent on Russian energy, it is all but inevitable that Russia will gain a greater influence over key European foreign policy decisions. The power of Arab and Iranian oil has already tilted European foreign policy away from Israel and made the European powers reluctant to approve meaningful sanctions on the Iranian regime in response to the ayatollahs' nuclear development program. We see the same dynamic in Sudan, where the power of Sudanese oil has made China (which buys two-thirds of Sudan's oil exports) Sudan's primary international defender, blocking numerous attempts in the UN Security Council and other international forums to punish the Sudanese government for its mass murder of its own people.

In the near future, we can expect Russia to try to use its natural resource leverage to loosen Europe's political and, especially, military ties to America. Russia opposes key American policies in Europe on a number of issues, including the independence of Kosovo and the installation in Europe of a U.S.-sponsored ballistic missile shield. A reduction in Russian energy supplies, or even just a rise in prices, is something Europeans will have to factor in to their foreign policy decisions as a potential cost of crossing Russia.

Putin, when president, made the risible argument that Russia had no intention of using energy supplies as a tool of foreign policy. Gazprom is a state-owned company, which means it does not operate according to the profit motive. Instead, it is an arm of the Russian state, run to advance Russian interests, and is ultimately responsible to the Russian president—the same man who sets the country's foreign policy agenda. It should come as no surprise, then, that several former KGB officials sit on Gazprom's board of directors, while state-controlled Rosneft is chaired by an ex-KGB agent who also serves as deputy chief of the Kremlin staff.[15]

In fact, the Kremlin has already begun throwing its new geopolitical weight around Europe. In April 2008, NATO members failed to reach an agreement to move the former Soviet republics of Georgia and Ukraine toward NATO membership. Although Canada, Eastern European nations, and Central European nations joined the United States in supporting NATO expansion, Russia vociferously opposed the move. Ultimately, France and Germany blocked expansion, fearing it could damage their ties with Russia. Sources close to the discussions told me they believe that Russia, implicitly or explicitly, threatened to cut off France and Germany's oil and gas supplies. Thus, through its energy leverage over Western European countries, Russia has apparently gained near-veto power over the very composition of the NATO alliance. When Russia invaded Georgia, the London *Times* ran a story with the headline, "Diplomats Warn Conflict Could Scupper Nato Membership Bid," which aptly captured NATO's position.[16] In other words, tough luck, Georgia, you might need NATO's shield, but we're not inviting anyone in who gets invaded by Russia.

When a state gets the kind of power over other nations that Russia has gained through its energy domination of Europe, it's very rare that it won't use it. But most likely, Russia will never have to actually wield its energy weapon. Cutting off European energy would be so damaging to France and Germany that, as we see with the negotiations over NATO expansion, the mere threat of it will suffice to make these ostensible American allies do Russia's bidding.

THE BIG PICTURE

We need to realize that the world is moving away from international free trade in energy. Instead of an energy trade based largely on supply and demand, supplies and prices are going to be dictated by the national interests of energy producing countries. State-owned oil companies now control approximately three-quarters of international oil reserves, and this proportion could rise further as more governments move to harness the wealth and power that control over natural resources can bring. Although liberals like to blame high oil prices on the alleged rapacity of America's independent oil companies, such companies, in fact, control just one-tenth of the world's proven hydrocarbon reserves. State-owned oil companies are by far the dominant player in the international energy trade, and it's they who exert the most power over questions of supply, production, and prices.[17]

In the future, countries that cooperate with the foreign policy goals of major suppliers like Venezuela and Russia will be rewarded with plentiful supplies and reasonable prices, while states that defy them will quickly find themselves paying exorbitant rates for oil and natural gas—if they're not cut off altogether. And control of energy supplies brings more than just diplomatic influence—massive dollar-denominated payments for oil supplies allow energy producers to accumulate huge dollar reserves that can be used to manipulate the value of the dollar and cause mischief in U.S. capital markets. And of course, all those dollars can be used to buy tanks, missiles, combat aircraft, and other weapons that only further enhance these countries' power.

The trend away from international free trade in energy presents a direct challenge to our well-being and our influence in the world. When so many major energy suppliers are openly hostile to the United States (Venezuela, Iran) or potentially hostile (Russia, the Arab states), it is the height of folly for us not to exploit our own reserves of energy. As others have noted, we are likely heading into a world of "resource wars"—a world for which America, right now, is woefully unprepared.[18]

★ ★ ★

CHAPTER 4

MAKING AMERICA ENERGY INDEPENDENT

D O YOU THINK PRESIDENT OBAMA IS THE RIGHT MAN TO COUNTER the growing threat of energy blackmail and to secure America's energy supplies in an increasingly hostile international climate? I fear that Obama and the congressional Democrats are neither tough enough nor practical enough to do what needs to be done. Instead, they seem intent on diverting America into pursuing costly and ultimately fruitless "green" sources of energy. That won't cut it.

We need a new, nationalist energy policy that harnesses both government power and private industry to achieve the crucial national goal of energy independence. The biggest domestic obstacle we face is liberals like President Obama with their petulant opposition to drilling for oil off our shores and in Alaska, with their superstitious fear of nuclear power, and with their emotional, apocalyptic belief in global warming that has created a mania for cutting our carbon emissions—even to the point of bankrupting our entire coal industry. When it comes to energy policy, the Democratic Party is hostage to environmental extremists. This is an issue on which they deserve a fight for the good of the country.

THE ALTERNATIVE ENERGY BOONDOGGLE

Liberals regard alternative energy as the magic solution to our dependence on foreign energy. The Obama campaign in particular was enthralled with its own utopian plan to create millions of "green collar jobs." Even the Bush Administration supported a number of alternative energy schemes, especially through its giant subsidies for ethanol production. The problem, however, is that every form of alternative energy—and even all of them combined—is hopelessly inadequate in meeting the needs of our economy.

Alternative energy is often presented as a panacea for our energy problems. If we can only find some substitute for oil, the thinking goes, we could simultaneously break our reliance on Middle Eastern suppliers and guarantee a clean, plentiful source of fuel. The search for a viable alternative energy already has an air of unreality about it, as if there's some magical fuel elixir that has not yet been developed because of a massive market failure in the American economy. But the truth is, while government subsidies for potential alternative energies may stimulate a certain amount of additional research, you can bet these funds pale in comparison to the massive windfall that awaits any entrepreneur or company that discovers a cheap, clean oil substitute. There is already more than enough market incentive to develop alternative energy.

The reason why no one has discovered a practical alternative energy is because none currently exists. Of course, any contribution from alternative energy would be welcome, but we have to be realistic about what alternative energy can really achieve: it might reduce our oil consumption at the margins. We simply can't expect anything more than that. And we must be aware of the damaging consequences of overemphasizing the possibilities of alternative energy.

For example, consider ethanol, the latest trendy oil alternative. Convinced that this corn-based alcohol fuel can reduce our dependence on foreign oil while helping to fight global warming, Congress has continually ratcheted up incentives and subsidies for the product; currently, ethanol producers save billions of dollars a year through a 51-cent per gallon ethanol tax break, while also benefiting from Congress's 2005 mandate to double the amount of renewable fuels—comprised almost exclusively of ethanol—used in gasoline to 8 billion gallons a year by 2012. In his 2007 State of the Union address, President Bush advocated nearly quintupling this target by 2017.

Ethanol, however, carries numerous drawbacks even aside from the billions of dollars in taxpayer subsidies. The government's massive support for ethanol has skewed the market as farmers have diverted 20 percent of America's corn crop to ethanol production. This has decreased the supply of corn, tripled corn prices since 2006, raised the price of everything from corn on the cob to feed for farm animals, and sparked the biggest rise in food prices in nearly two decades at the beginning of 2008.[1]

The international situation is no better; in an internal report, the World Bank reports that biofuels have sparked a 75 percent increase in food prices.[2] This has led to food riots or grain rationing in Bangladesh, Egypt, and other countries. The UN Food and Agriculture Organization is now calling for an international review of biofuel subsidies as a potential enemy of the world's poor and hungry.[3]

Moreover, the government's massive ethanol program will hardly dent our oil consumption. As energy journalist and author Robert Bryce notes,

[Eight] billion gallons of ethanol will do almost nothing to reduce our oil imports. Eight billion gallons may sound like a lot, until you realize that America burned more than 134 billion gallons of gasoline [in 2004]. By 2012, those 8 billion gallons might reduce America's overall oil consumption by 0.5 percent. Way back in 1997, the General Accounting Office concluded that "ethanol's potential for substituting for petroleum is so small that it is unlikely to significantly affect overall energy security." That's still true today.[4]

Even if we hit former President Bush's extravagant target of using 35 billion gallons of ethanol by 2017, this would likely amount to no more than 3.5 percent of our oil usage, or just slightly more than the amount of gas we'd save if, as George Will pointed out, drivers properly inflated their tires.[5]

There is a lesson to be learned from the ethanol debacle. The environmentalists and other true believers who advocated ethanol thought they had found a "carbon-neutral" fuel source that could reduce global warming, but they didn't anticipate that their policies would result in food riots. And they probably never realized or accepted that ethanol, at best, has an extremely limited role to play in our national energy usage. Nevertheless, there's still a lot of support for biofuels among global warming alarmists. Barack Obama and Joe Biden even campaigned on a vow to "require at least 60 billion gallons of advanced biofuels by 2030." And how will they do this? By investing "federal resources, including tax incentives and government contracts, into developing the most promising technologies and building the infrastructure to support them."[6] Apparently, much more expensive food for the world's poor is an acceptable price to pay for liberals to feel like they're "doing something" about global warming.

Other forms of alternative energy look even less promising. Hydropower, which accounts for nearly 80 percent of America's renewable energy, is severely limited by the location of suitable water sources. It also requires dam building that can destroy local wildlife and river ecosystems, flood valuable crop land, and even force mass evacuations—like the 4 million souls who will have to be relocated as part of China's Three Gorges Dam project.[7]

Other sources of renewable energy don't even merit serious consideration as major sources of power. Farmers would need more than 1,500 miles of highly-productive land to harvest enough biomass to match the output of one nuclear power plant; wind farms would have to blanket an area the size of Texas and Louisiana to meet America's electricity demand; and solar energy remains grossly inefficient, with no significant technological breakthroughs in the last thirty years.[8] As a CATO study notes, wind and solar power constitute less than 1 percent of domestic electricity, and probably wouldn't exist at all if not for the government subsidies they've enjoyed for three decades.[9] In perhaps the best example of the exaggerated hopes for alternative energy, wind power enthusiast T. Boone Pickens in November 2008 suspended his grandiose plan to spend billions of dollars to build the world's largest wind farm—because he found it was not economically viable at the time.[10]

Hopes for a profitable electric car are proving equally unfounded. GM's Chevy Volt—a plug-in hybrid scheduled to hit the market in late 2010—is often touted as the first step in our inevitable transition to battery-operated cars. In order to cover the cost of the battery and other green features, however, the vehicle will be priced at around $40,000, which guarantees few people would buy it without the huge government incentives that have already been approved. But successfully selling the car could be even worse for GM—the company already admits that the Volt will not be profitable. As the *Atlantic*'s in-depth report on the Volt found, "Unless battery costs fall as quickly as GM hopes, the car could break the bank by succeeding."[11]

While various political, business, and environmental interests always maintain that some transformative technological breakthrough is just around the corner, energy's magic bullet never appears. As a result, many liberals and environmentalists argue that we need a national effort to conserve our scarce energy. But the fact is, of course, that individuals and industries are already motivated to use energy as efficiently as possible, because it costs money— when energy becomes scarce it becomes more expensive, and people use less of it. So the free market imposes energy efficiency much more effectively than public service campaigns and liberal hectoring ever will. That doesn't, however, solve our problem.

We need a tremendous amount of energy to propel the economy forward. Historically, there is a direct correlation between energy use and economic activity—and thus prosperity. In other words, when it comes to energy, it's impossible for a country to conserve its way to greater prosperity. Alternative energy is not the answer either, notwithstanding the near-utopian liberal claims about its potential.

The future, like the present, belongs to fossil fuels—oil, coal, and natural gas. These have powered modern economies since the Industrial Revolution, and now account for approximately 86 percent of our energy consumption (40 percent for oil and 23 percent each for coal and natural gas),[12] a percentage that is expected to remain constant for years to come. To bring us that energy, oil, coal, and natural gas companies take great risks, including huge investments in often turbulent parts of the world. For this, they are demonized by the left. In fact, Obama has promised to slap a windfall tax on what he calls "excessive oil company profits,"[13] as if oil companies deserve to be punished for doing their job well and achieving the profits they need to fund future oil, gas, and coal exploration.

Like it or not, we need oil, we need lots of it, and we will continue to rely on it for the rest of our lifetimes.

DRILL, BABY, DRILL? YOU BETCHA

In the meantime, foreign oil supplies are likely to become even more precarious as hostile states use oil as a foreign policy weapon pointed at America. And we are vulnerable to this blackmail due to our rising dependence on foreign oil—our output of crude oil fell 43 percent between 1985 and 2005, while demand increased 31 percent, resulting in 200 percent growth in net imports of petroleum products.[14]

Since alternative energies will not wean us off foreign oil, our only option is to expand our own oil production. We took a step in this direction in 2008, when both Congress and President Bush finally allowed the bans on off-shore oil drilling to expire. Public fury drove them to this, and the anger was justified; America's outer-continental shelf holds an estimated 115 billion barrels of oil.[15]

The crucial issue of how much drilling will be allowed will be set by President Obama and the new Congress. And the initial signals are worrying: liberal lawmakers clearly wanted to maintain the drilling ban, but their hands were forced during an election year. Obama was also half-hearted in supporting the expansion of off-shore drilling, framing it as a "compromise" necessary for the approval of various alternative energy programs.[16] So it's a good bet that any expansion of off-shore drilling under the Obama administration will be kept to a symbolic minimum.

Moreover, as my old boss Newt Gingrich notes, we can expect that new drilling projects will be tied up for years by frivolous legal challenges from environmental organizations.[17] Since expanding our oil production is now a national security matter, we need to counter this with a federal law establishing special energy courts to adjudicate these challenges quickly. These courts, like our intelligence courts, should be staffed by judges with expertise in the issues over which they're presiding. Once a drilling project or a nuclear plant is approved at the federal level, opponents would be given an administrative hearing and then one appeal to a designated appellate court. If they lose the appeal, the litigation ends and the project moves forward. This is the only way to pre-empt what will surely be a concerted campaign of anti-drilling guerrilla legal actions at the local, state, and federal levels.

We can strike the right balance between legitimate environmental concerns and energy security. But where it's a close call, we should err on behalf of our national security needs. This holds true in Alaska, where there is an estimated mean 7.7 billion barrels of technically recoverable oil in the 1002 area of the Arctic National Wildlife Refuge (ANWAR). [18] This is America's most promising untapped onshore oil field. It needs to be opened to drilling, and it could be done with minimal damage to the surrounding habitat.

We also need to exploit fully our resources of natural gas. An estimated 200 trillion cubic feet of undiscovered, recoverable natural gas exists in the Gulf of Mexico, an amount that exceeds the entire proved natural gas reserves of the United States. Until recently, however, drilling in some of the most promising areas off the Florida coast was banned because of pressure from environmentalists and local Florida politicians.[19] Now that some of these bans have been lifted, we need to take full advantage of this vital national resource.

Oil shale holds even more promise. Shale is a sedimentary rock that, when heated to extreme temperatures, yields hydrocarbons that can be transformed into a fuel source suitable for use as jet fuel or diesel, and can also be turned into gasoline. The downside of oil shale is that it's relatively expensive to extract and refine, and the process carries environmental challenges. The upside, however, is attention-grabbing: in just three western states, the U.S. has the estimated equivalent of 1.8 trillion barrels of oil—nearly *seven times* the proved oil reserves of Saudi Arabia.[20]

These massive oil shale deposits are located along the Green River Formation that stretches across Colorado, Wyoming, and Utah. Despite a few experimental projects in the past and a handful of ongoing R&D projects, these deposits remain largely untapped because, until recently, the low price of oil meant that oil shale could not be extracted profitably. Government as well as private oil shale projects picked up when the price of oil spiked after the 1973 oil embargo, then disbanded when oil prices dropped in the early 1980s.[21] Today, there is no commercial oil shale production in the United States.

There are several problems hindering oil shale production. Like most oil extraction methods, the processing of shale can have negative environmental impacts such as groundwater contamination. These problems are by no means insurmountable for a company willing to spend the money needed to keep its shale extraction methods relatively clean; Shell has already engineered some environmental breakthroughs in shale extraction. A bigger impediment to oil shale production, however, is the high price of extracting it. Because the product is more difficult than crude oil to remove from the ground, and it takes additional processes to turn it into gasoline, oil shale is significantly more expensive to produce than crude. While a barrel of crude costs just a few dollars to produce under optimum conditions in the Middle East, and between $15 and $25 in the United States, oil shale can cost $50 per barrel or even more.

The expense of production and extraction, however, is a problem that is already being solved. Rising global demand and rising prices will make oil shale profitable, and advances in technology will cut oil shale production costs. For example, Shell, which is one of the few companies currently exploring oil shale production in Colorado, is developing an in situ conversion technique that heats the shale while still in the ground. To prevent groundwater contamination, Shell builds an ice barrier around the production area. The company estimates that its production model can be profitable with oil prices as low as $30 per barrel.[22] If prices stay at current levels or, more likely, rise steadily in the future, this will become a lucrative enterprise that other oil companies will be tempted to replicate.

A final barrier to large-scale oil shale production is that around three-quarters of the Green River shale deposits are located on land owned by the federal government, where shale exploration, until recently, was mostly banned. The government needs to rapidly and generously lease these areas out for oil shale projects. Although some private land is available, the government-owned tracts tend to sit upon the thickest and richest shale deposits. What's more, companies wanting to start up oil shale projects navigate a byzantine permitting process requiring dozens of permissions from the local, state, and federal levels.[23] Such bureaucratic hindrances have got to go. The federal government needs to fast-track oil shale production with the same sense of urgency that animated the Manhattan Project because oil shale production will take time—a RAND study estimated a firm would need at least twelve years for an oil shale project to reach the production growth phase.[24]

This being the case, the government needs to offer incentives for private companies to move into oil shale production immediately. Guaranteeing a price of around $50 per barrel would encourage companies to make big, long-term investments in oil shale.

In 2008, Congress allowed the ban on oil shale exploration in the Green River Formation to expire. But now, it's all in the hands of President Obama and the Democratic Congress, which means the prospects for oil shale development are grim. Democrats were even more reluctant to allow oil shale development than they were offshore drilling, as evidenced by Senator Harry Reid's sneaky attempt to renew the oil shale exploration ban as part of the legislation for the financial bailout.[25] What's more, a coalition of eleven environmental groups is already threatening to sue the Interior Department to stall oil shale projects.[26]

If you want to know what's preventing the United States from achieving energy independence, you need look no further than the environmentalists and liberals who are always erecting new obstacles to energy production. They're all in favor of throwing taxpayer dollars at alternative energy sources that will never work, but will do everything in their power to block us from tapping our enormous supply of oil shale, as well as our rich deposits of offshore and onshore crude oil, unless the American people at large, and the Republican Party in particular, force their hand.

GLOBAL WARMING

Fears of global warming already play an important role in our energy policy. These concerns will ultimately disappear, because the very idea of "catastrophic manmade global warming" will eventually be debunked, as environmental doomsday scenarios always are. But for now, global warming has emerged as the new cause célèbre of the environmental movement, replacing all the previous alarmist predictions of the imminent depletion of natural resources, uncontrollable population growth, and even global cooling.

According to global warmists, the average rise in the Earth's temperature of around 1 degree in the last century is a harbinger of doom for mankind. They predict temperatures will rise by a few more degrees over the next century, leading to catastrophic environmental occurrences such as droughts and coastal flooding. In *An Inconvenient Truth*, Al Gore hypothesizes a twenty-foot rise in sea levels due to global warming. Scientist James Lovelock lovingly predicted that "before this century is over billions of us will die and the few breeding pairs of people that survive will be in the Arctic where the climate remains tolerable."[27] Not to be outdone, CNN founder Ted Turner envisions an even bleaker future: "Not [fighting global warming] will be catastrophic. We'll be eight degrees hotter in 30 or 40 years and basically none of the crops will grow.... Most of the people will have died and the rest of us will be cannibals."[28]

Instead of moderating the hysterical tone of the debate, Barack Obama has enthusiastically added to it. On the first page of his official environmental plan, he warns of environmental catastrophe on a biblical scale unless we adopt his policies:

> We cannot afford more of the same timid politics when the future of our planet is at stake. Global warming is not a someday problem, it is now. We are already breaking records with the intensity of our storms, the number of forest fires, the periods of drought. By 2050 famine could force more than 250 million from their homes .... The polar ice caps are now melting faster than science had ever predicted.... This is not the future I want for my daughters. It's not the future any of us want for our children. And if we act now and we act boldly, it doesn't have to be.[29]

Although global warmers claim a scientific consensus backs their views on the issue, a lot of the projections are based on a near-religious faith in the accuracy of immensely complex models used to predict future global temperatures. Even the global warming alarmists of the UN's Intergovernmental Panel on Climate Change acknowledge "significant deficiencies" in these kinds of models, including "large differences" in how models respond when testing the same variables believed to cause climate change.[30]

Despite such scientific uncertainties, global warmists cling to their theories as if they were handed down to Al Gore on Mt. Sinai—or perhaps Gore thinks he was the one handing down the truth to man. When evidence arises that contradicts the warming creed, the data are simply shunted aside or dismissed as some bizarre anomaly. In March 2008, for example, National Public Radio revealed that a fleet of 3,000 scientific robots placed in the ocean in 2003 to measure oceanic temperatures were reporting that over the last five years the ocean, instead of warming, has slightly *cooled*. In an article comically titled "The Mystery of Global Warming's Missing Heat," NPR speculated that the cooling trend "could mean global warming has taken a breather. Or it could mean scientists aren't quite understanding what their robots are telling them."[31] The article quotes scientists offering various theories about the "mysterious" and "puzzling" missing heat. The notion that the readings really mean that the ocean just hasn't gotten any warmer in the last few years apparently didn't occur to anyone. This finding should really come as no surprise since, contrary to conventional wisdom, average global temperatures have not actually risen at all since 1998.[32]

The scientific case against global warming is most cogently explained in *Unstoppable Global Warming Every 1,500 Years*. In this book, academic researchers S. Fred Singer and Dennis Avery argue that current weather patterns are a normal part of a 1,500 year warming and cooling cycle that has affected the planet for a million years. The authors meticulously debunk the predictions of a coming climactic Armageddon, noting that a slightly warming planet would not cause any of the natural catastrophes predicted by Gore and Co. In fact, Singer and Avery observe that a moderately warmer planet would be beneficial in many ways, for example by allowing for increased agricultural production and more wildlife biodiversity.[33] Danish academic Bjørn Lomborg adds the much-overlooked point that if the globe slightly warms up, heat-related deaths will be more than offset by an even greater decline in the number of deaths from cold—a warming planet is projected to save an incredible 1.7 million lives a year by 2050.[34]

In many ways, global warming has become a moral crusade impervious to standard analyses of costs and benefits. Natural disasters are now interpreted as Mother Nature exacting righteous retribution on fuel-addicted humans who stubbornly refuse to listen to environmentalists. In blaming Hurricane Katrina on global warming, environmental activist Robert F. Kennedy declared, "Now we are all learning what it's like to reap the whirlwind of fossil fuel dependence."[35] Those who question the scientific basis of the global warmists' extravagant threats are treated not as cautious skeptics, but rather as nefarious heretics. Al Gore compared them to people who believe that the Earth is flat and that NASA faked the moon landings.[36]

The alarmists want to bind America to international treaties like the Kyoto Protocol that would commit us to reduce our fossil fuel emissions, even though the estimated cost of America's compliance with Kyoto would be an astounding $325 billion, for a benefit that is utterly unproven.[37] Bjørn Lomborg, who believes in manmade global warming, points out that cutting greenhouse gas emissions "actually is one of the least helpful ways of serving humanity or the environment." Dispassionately analyzing the Kyoto Protocol in his book, *Cool It*, he estimates that U.S. compliance would entail huge costs for "almost trivial benefits." At best, Lomborg concludes, if every nation signed up for Kyoto and upheld its commitments for the entire twenty-first century, it would affect the temperature by a mere 0.3 degrees Fahrenheit by 2100.[38]

While they didn't get Kyoto signed, global warmists have reason for optimism, since Barack Obama supports a mandatory "cap-and-trade" system that is little more than a disguised carbon tax that would impose enormous costs on U.S. industry. Since emissions cuts actually have minimal effect on the weather, as Lomborg demonstrates, there can be little doubt that once emissions cuts are forced on our industries, environmentalists will point to their ineffectiveness as proof that even more drastic cuts are needed to fight the global warming bogeyman.

While dramatically cutting our use of fossil fuels might make environmentalists feel good, the crippling effect on our economy will make most working Americans feel otherwise. Liberals know this, so they conceal their real policies. For example, in arguing for a worldwide carbon tax, *Atlantic Monthly* senior editor Clive Crook makes the following remarkable proposal:

> Many U.S. politicians see a carbon tax as electoral poison, regardless of the new mood on climate change. Maybe they're right—but political resistance to an explicit tax need not block this approach. One could simply link the carbon tax to an equivalent cut in some other tax. Alternatively, systems that disguise carbon taxes from the public are easy to devise, and the details could be left to individual countries.

For instance, a modified cap-and-trade system (with additional permits for sale at a fixed price) could mimic the carbon-curbing effects of a tax.[39]

Of course, a cap-and-trade system is exactly what Obama has in store for us. That activists need to "disguise" their true policies from the public speaks to the profoundly antidemocratic nature of the global warming movement. While American environmentalists might derive a certain naïve satisfaction in sacrificing America's own national interests for the sake of a global campaign to fight a nonexistent enemy, I propose a different course—one that puts America first.

NUCLEAR ENERGY

Besides tapping our domestic oil reserves, we need to make even more use of coal, which is now our largest source of energy after oil. We have huge coal reserves—enough to last for at least another hundred years at current consumption rates, according to the National Petroleum Council.[40] Since clean coal technology is already very advanced, we should be moving full speed ahead to bring even more coal online. This is the precise opposite course of the one signaled by President Obama who, while magnanimously conceding that we can't totally eliminate the use of coal, has vowed to make any company's construction of a new coal plant so costly that "it will bankrupt them."[41]

Likewise, the United States has an abundance of natural gas that almost makes us self-sufficient. In order to provide for future growth in population and energy usage, we need to continue the search for new domestic gas sources, particularly in the outer continental shelf off Florida. Active exploration of Green River shale will also increase our supply of natural gas, which is a byproduct of the shale extraction process.

Additionally, there is one major source of energy that should be much more widely used—nuclear energy. Cheap, clean, and safe, nuclear power is a crucial element of the U.S. energy mix, providing around 20 percent of our total electricity. But nuclear energy is severely underutilized thanks to the same kind of environmental alarmism that is blocking oil shale exploration.

This is largely a result of successful agitation by the anti-nuclear movement. This particular crusade arose alongside the environmental movement of the 1960s. Touting the alleged environmental dangers of nuclear power, the movement pressed for the abolition of nuclear power plants. Activists argued that nuclear energy was unsafe and posed a direct environmental threat, although some of them had ulterior motives for opposing nuclear power. When asked about the prospects of nuclear fission in 1977, an influential leader of the anti-nuclear movement, Amory Lovins, replied, "If you ask me, it'd be a little short of disastrous for us to discover a source of clean, cheap, abundant energy because of what we would do with it. We ought to be looking for energy sources that are adequate for our needs, but that won't give us the excesses of concentrated energy with which we could do mischief to the earth or to each other."[42]

Similar sentiments were expressed by Paul Ehrlich, who is most famous for his 1968 book *The Population Bomb*, in which he made the spectacularly misguided prediction that population growth would inevitably result in an unprecedented worldwide famine in the 1970s and 1980s. In a 1978 article on nuclear power, Ehrlich wrote, "Giving society cheap, abundant energy...would be the equivalent of giving an idiot child a machine gun."[43]

Thus, some prominent early environmentalists opposed nuclear energy specifically *because* it is a clean, cheap, plentiful source of energy. Viewing humankind as a destructive "idiot child," they feared nuclear energy would allow for greater technological progress—a mortal sin in their eyes that results in ever more pillaging of the environment. Such activists represent the Luddite wing of the environmental movement which, unfortunately, tends to have an outsized voice in the media when it comes to the public debate over energy issues.

The accidents at the Three Mile Island nuclear power plant near Harrisburg, Pennsylvania, in 1979 and at Chernobyl in 1986 helped the anti-nuclear movement spread a popular fear of nuclear power. To our detriment, new construction of American nuclear power plants slowed and eventually stopped altogether; no new nuclear plants have opened in America for over a decade.

This trend is not only harmful to our energy security, but it's based on wild exaggerations of the risks of nuclear power. In all the passionate commentary on the Three Mile Island accident, for example, not only is it forgotten that there were no deaths associated with the partial core meltdown at the plant, but there were not even any injuries or measurable health impacts to the general public at all. This was borne out by a Pennsylvania Department of Health registry of over 30,000 people who lived within five miles of the plant at the time of the accident. After eighteen years, the registry terminated without finding any evidence of adverse health trends due to the accident.[44]

The famous Chernobyl meltdown is the only accident at a civilian nuclear power plant *anywhere* that caused fatalities among the general public. What's more, reports of tens of thousands of deaths due to Chernobyl were dismissed as gross exaggerations in a major study commissioned by the International Atomic Energy Agency (IAEA), which found that the radiation doses affecting the general population were "relatively low," resulting in a few thousand additional cases of thyroid cancer.[45] Nevertheless, the Chernobyl meltdown became public exhibit number one in the anti-nuclear movement's campaign, with anti-nuclear groups like Greenpeace warning darkly of the possibility of "an American Chernobyl."[46]

Today, the most valid environmental concern associated with nuclear power is the disposal of spent nuclear fuel. This issue, however, is already a matter of concern even if no new nuclear power plants are constructed. Without a permanent site to deposit radioactive rods, many nuclear power plants keep them on-site in temporary storage containers. While these containers are safe from an environmental standpoint, for security and efficiency's sake, it would be preferable to find a single permanent storage site. After extensive studies, the government found a suitable location 1,000 feet below ground at Nevada's Yucca Mountain. But resistance from Nevada politicians, including Senate Majority leader Harry Reid, has stymied the project.

It's understandable that Nevadans, responding to irrational public fears, would prefer any location for the site other than their own back yard. However, Yucca Mountain is safe and must be made operational. Storing spent fuel at Yucca would increase the safety and security of existing nuclear power plants, as well as future ones that could contribute vital energy to the American economy. In accepting the Yucca site, Nevadans would make a vital contribution to our energy security, which has become inextricably tied to our overall national security. Nevadans are not being asked to lay down their lives for their country, as hundreds of thousands of Americans have done throughout our history. But they are being asked to give up their unjustified fears.

Thankfully, the Bush Administration took a new look at nuclear energy and approved tax breaks and other incentives to encourage nuclear power production. This was a much-needed reversal in government policy toward nuclear energy.

The future of nuclear power, however, is in doubt because Barack Obama is far from a nuclear power enthusiast. He has conceded that nuclear power produces less carbon than other forms of energy, but he warns that storage, security, waste, and proliferation issues must be addressed before an expansion of nuclear power can even be considered.[47] He opposes Yucca Mountain as a nuclear storage site, and his administration is really promising that years will pass before it will even contemplate expanding nuclear power.

This is sadly representative of Obama's entire outlook on energy policy. He promises to punish producers of oil, natural gas, and nuclear power—the only sources of energy that work—through windfall profit taxes, cap-and-trade schemes, and the like, while rewarding "alternative" energies that don't.

If we start promptly with a sense of urgency, minimal price guarantees, and a streamlined approval process, within a decade America could be producing extraordinary levels of fuel from oil shale. We would be moving, year by year, quickly toward not only energy independence, but eventually energy surplus. The technology is available and market conditions will support unlimited production. Only politics stands in the way.

Once we have reached these objectives, we will be in the enviable geopolitical position of being, like Russia and Saudi Arabia today, an exporter of oil and refined gasoline. It will be an invaluable tool of our foreign policy and our national interest.

It is inexcusable that our politicians—and particularly the Democratic Congress and President Obama—refuse, as a matter of ideological opposition to carbon-based energy production, to permit this sure path to vastly increased national security. It would appear that as long as the current government is in office, America will continue to be exposed to the most dangerous risks to our national security and economic vitality. And, while this government clearly has the legal authority to refuse to enact such a policy, it is also undeniable that its policy of denying America a reliable, independent source of abundant energy empowers our sworn enemies to take ravenous advantage of the American people.

History will surely file the harshest possible verdict against the current government if it continues this course. President Obama and his Democratic Party cohorts, by their blind refusal to provide for the common interest and defense, demonstrate the triumph of ideology over national security.[48]

CHAPTER 5

★   ★   ★

IN PRAISE OF
CENSORSHIP

MANY YEARS AGO IN A CLASSIC ESSAY, IRVING KRISTOL WROTE, "IF you care for the quality of life in our American democracy, then you have to be for censorship." Kristol was writing about obscenity and pornography. My purpose here is different. I am talking about censorship in wartime—and we are, lest we forget, at war.

During wartime, there is a natural tension between civil liberties and national security, but security must take precedence. I don't propose any novel legal interpretations to get us to the right balance between civil liberties and national security, only a return to America's wartime traditions. The politically incorrect fact is that America's history teaches us that curtailments on civil liberties help to win wars, and we need far stricter laws to guard our national security secrets.

THE THREAT WE FACE

After the terrorist attacks of September 11, 2001, the Bush administration rolled back very few civil liberties. Aside from establishing a regime for handling captured foreign terrorists, the curtailments largely consisted of common-sense enhancements in the power of intelligence agencies to monitor terrorism suspects and access their personal records. And the administration did so, in a limited way, because it rightly deemed these restrictions in America's national security interests. Bush's steps were modest, yet liberal journalists reacted as if he were the reincarnation of Stalin, or, more to their taste, Hitler.

- Writer Michael Kinsley asserted that "in terms of the power he now claims, without significant challenge, George W. Bush is now the closest thing in a long time to dictator of the world."
- *Newsweek* columnist Jonathan Alter proclaimed, "We're seeing clearly now that Bush thought 9/11 gave him license to act like a dictator."
- *American Prospect* editor Robert Kuttner accused the Bush administration of engineering "a slow-rolling coup d'etat."
- CNN commentator Jack Cafferty argued that Senator Arlen Specter, who led an inquiry into reports of the National Security Agency's investigation of domestic telephone records, "might be all that's standing between us and a full-blown dictatorship in this country."
- U.S. Court of Appeals judge Guido Calabresi claimed the Supreme Court's adjudication of the 2000 election was "exactly what happened" when Mussolini and Hitler seized power. He added that, like Mussolini, Bush "has

exercised extraordinary power—he has exercised power, claimed power for himself."[1]

These jeremiads complement a healthy market in books that make the same argument, such as Charlie Savage's *Takeover: The Return of the Imperial Presidency and the Subversion of American Democracy*. In another such tome, *It Can Happen Here: Authoritarian Peril in the Age of Bush*, Joe Conason ominously warns: "For the first time since the resignation of Richard M. Nixon more than three decades ago, Americans have had reason to doubt the future of democracy and the rule of law in our own country. Today we live in a state of tension between the enjoyment of traditional freedoms, including the protections afforded to speech and person by the Bill of Rights, and the disturbing realization that those freedoms have been undermined and may be abrogated at any moment."[2]

These diatribes against the new American autocracy show an embarrassing ignorance of the history of executive authority. The government's power, and especially that of the executive branch, has traditionally expanded during wartime, when the country has faced all manner of foreign and internal threats. In fact, the expansion of government power since the September 11 attacks pales in comparison to the kinds of authority exerted by past U.S. presidents during wartime. Today, far from enjoying dictatorial powers, the president faces inordinate constraints that hinder the government's effectiveness in protecting us from the threat of Islamic terrorism. One ironic outcome of the 2008 election is that liberals will no doubt abandon their warnings now that it's Barack Obama who enjoys that "dictatorial" power.

Of course, some observers reject outright the necessity of enhanced government powers. Denying that we are currently in a time of national peril, some argue that Islamist fascism does not present an existential threat to America. Government counterterrorism consultant Mark Sageman argues in his 2008 book, *Leaderless Jihad*, that global Islamic terrorists represent merely a "small threat" and a "self-limiting" one that should be "contained" until it "fade[s] away":

> In devising a strategy, it is important to understand whether the danger the United States faces is in fact a threat to the existence of the nation. The Soviet Union had thousands of nuclear missiles poised at the United States, ready to destroy the entire country within a few hours. This is definitely not the case with global Islamist terrorism. September 11, despite being an atrocity and the largest single terrorist event in world history, did not come close to wiping out the United States. Even the worst imaginable event, a biological or a nuclear strike by terrorists, will not destroy the nation. In fact, at this point in history, only the United States could obliterate the United States.[3]

Of course, the view of Islamic terrorists as a nuisance properly handled by law enforcement, with no need for any enhanced government powers, was one of the primary reasons why the threat was allowed to grow for so many years, despite numerous warnings, leading up to September 11. Since then, Americans have fallen into a deep sense of complacency. After September 11, the government encouraged us to go about our daily lives and leave the battle against Islamic terrorism entirely up to our troops fighting in far away lands.

It is a sobering experience, then, to read of the 2008 Senate hearings on the threat of a nuclear attack on a U.S. city and the possible response scenarios. Here's how the *Washington Times* described a hearing of the Senate panel:

> A nuclear device detonated near the White House would kill roughly 100,000 people and flatten downtown federal buildings, while the radioactive plume from the explosion would likely spread toward the Capitol and into Southeast D.C., contaminating thousands more.

> The blast from the 10-kiloton bomb—similar to the bomb dropped over Hiroshima during World War II—would kill up to one in 10 tourists visiting the Washington Monument and send shards of glass flying the length of the National Mall, in a scenario that has become increasingly likely to occur in a major U.S. city in recent years, panel members told a Senate committee yesterday.

> "It's inevitable," said Cham E. Dallas, director of the Institute for Health Management and Mass Destruction Defense at the University of Georgia, who has charted the potential explosion's effect in the District and testified before a hearing of the Senate Committee on Homeland Security and Governmental Affairs. "I think it's wistful to think that it won't happen by 20 years."

> .... Ashton B. Carter, co-director of the Preventive Defense Project at Harvard University, said the likelihood of a nuclear attack on U.S. soil is undetermined, but it has increased with the proliferation of weapons by Iran and North Korea and the failure to secure Russia's nuclear arsenal following the Cold War.

"For while the probability of a nuclear weapon one day going off in a U.S. city cannot be calculated, it is almost surely larger than it was five years ago," Mr. Carter said.

. . . . Mr. Dallas said a major problem facing most cities is a lack of available hospital beds for victims of burns that would result from a nuclear blast. He said up to 95 percent of such victims would not receive potentially life-saving care.

"We're completely underprepared," he said. "Most of them will die."[4]

In a December 2008 draft report, a bipartisan, congressionally mandated commission found there was a better-than-even chance that terrorists would attack a major international city with weapons of mass destruction in the next few years. Analysts such as Sageman may take solace in the notion that America might survive such an attack, but I'd rather not see that supposition put to the test. The threat of some kind of nuclear device being detonated in America is greater now than it was during the Cold War, when the doctrine of mutually assured destruction ensured that no nuclear weapons were used in what we used to call the balance of terror. That was before A. Q. Khan developed Pakistan's nuclear weapons program and spread his knowhow to North Korea, Libya, Iran, and possibly other states. Khan's nuclear proliferation, which occurred alongside the spread of the poisonous doctrine of Islamic jihadism, makes American national security today more precarious than at any time since World War II, with the exception of the days of the Cuban Missile Crisis.

Yet some argue that mutually assured destruction will deter even an Islamic fundamentalist regime like Iran from using nuclear weapons or other weapons of mass destruction. This may, in fact, be true. But the argument ignores the more pressing question of whether Iran would give a suitcase nuke to a lone operative or terrorist group to use in America if the regime thought it could cover its tracks. Perhaps the mullahs would give such a weapon to an operative, along with instructions to pass it on to another person or group who is unknown to the regime. That way, the Iranians could truthfully testify after a nuke explodes in Washington D.C., New York City, or Los Angeles, that they have no idea who did it. Or maybe a rogue state like Syria, which had a surreptitious nuclear program in the works until the Israelis bombed its reactor site in September 2007, could secretly develop a nuke and pass it on to terrorists.

A hostile regime need not even develop nuclear weapons itself, if it can simply acquire them on the black market. North Korea, which was implicated in the secret Syrian nuclear program, has proven itself to be a dangerous proliferator. And as Ashton Carter indicated before the Senate, we can hardly trust the fidelity of those tasked with guarding nuclear weapons in Russia, a country consistently ranked near the top in global corruption surveys.[5]

The possibility of nuclear weapons falling into the hands of an Islamic terror group represents a serious threat to American security. And we must not ignore the very real possibility of another conventional terror strike. We now know that Islamic fundamentalists have been working hard to pull off additional spectacular attacks on America. These have only been avoided thanks to the hard work of Western intelligence services. In August 2006, a group of Islamic fanatics in Britain were implicated in a plot to blow up at least seven American-bound flights over the Atlantic Ocean. Nine months later, police arrested a jihadist cell planning to massacre U.S. soldiers at Fort Dix. In February 2008, the U.S. Transportation Security Administration reported that U.S. mass transit and rail systems are "vulnerable to terrorist attacks" and that despite the government's lack of intelligence on specific plans, terrorists "remain intent on targeting the U.S. homeland."[6] Islamic terrorists, whether armed with suitcase nukes or simple box cutters, must be treated as the grave security threat that they are, and not as common criminals who can be properly contained by our criminal justice system.

This means that the U.S. government must claim enhanced powers, as it traditionally has during wartime, in order to combat the threat of Islamic terrorism. To insist on the continuation of all the civil liberties we enjoyed during the 1990s is to handcuff the government in its war fighting efforts, making another terror attack more likely. As Judge Richard A. Posner notes,

> A military enemy can usually be fought with minimal impairment of civil liberties beyond conscription and the censorship of militarily sensitive information. But terrorists do not field military forces that we can grapple with in the open. And they are not content to operate against us abroad; they penetrate our country by stealth to kill us. Rooting out an invisible enemy in our midst might be fatally inhibited if we felt constrained to strict observance of civil liberties designed in and for eras in which the only serious internal threat (apart from spies) came from common criminals.[7]

The notion that civil liberties should contract during wartime and expand in peacetime is hardly revolutionary. As the late Supreme Court Chief Justice William Rehnquist wrote, "In any civilized society the most important task is achieving a proper balance between freedom and order. In wartime, reason and history both suggest that this balance shifts to some degree in favor of order—in favor of the government's ability to deal with conditions that threaten the national well-being."[8]

As a nation founded on freedom, and with constitutional protections for that freedom, and given our history, we know that temporary restrictions on civil liberties during wartime should be and will be temporary. However long the current war against Islamic fascism lasts, our history shows that our civil liberties, restricted in wartime, have always been fully reasserted once wartime danger has passed. Judge Posner observes, "The safer the nation feels, the greater the weight that the courts place on personal liberty relative to public safety. When the nation feels endangered, the balance shifts the other way."[9] This has traditionally been the natural and proper course of U.S. jurisprudence.

My argument is simply this: a temporary reduction of personal and media freedoms is an acceptable price to pay in order to lessen the chance that Islamic fanatics will commit further atrocities against the American people.

THE REAL HISTORY OF AMERICAN CENSORSHIP

In my previous book, *The West's Last Chance*, I outlined some of the powers assumed by the government under President Roosevelt during World War II. Primary among these powers was the authority FDR gave to FBI director J. Edgar Hoover to censor all news and communications entering or leaving America. A federal Office of Censorship was created to review and if necessary censor any criticism of the morale of U.S. forces, or any communication that might bring aid or comfort to the enemy. Censorship applied not only to news and commentary, but also popular entertainment. Anti-war films were all but unheard of, since the government simply would not allow them.

There is a marked contrast between that situation and what we see today, when the American public has been treated to a parade of Hollywood anti-war films, including *Rendition*, *Lions for Lambs*, *Stop Loss*, and *Redacted*, to name a few. Notwithstanding liberal hyperventilating over the supposed infringements on their right to "dissent," Americans remain free to denounce the government, the war effort, and the U.S. military in the most disparaging terms, which is typically what one sees in the antiwar rallies that occur every few months on the Washington mall, with the full permission of the authorities.

Notwithstanding his current status as a liberal icon, President Roosevelt was not particularly liberal about tolerating dissent during wartime, repeatedly asking his Attorney General, Francis Biddle, "When are you going to indict the seditionists?" Fascists, communists, and isolationists were prosecuted or denaturalized for speaking out against the war effort. Most notable among these repressions was the case against William Dudley Pelley, an isolationist and Nazi sympathizer who spent ten years in jail after being convicted of seditious libel for his denunciations of the war and of Roosevelt personally.[10]

At the beginning of World War II, around twenty-six news stories were censored in the American press every day; by the end of 1942, the Post Office had completely outlawed seventy newspapers.[11] Compare that restrictive environment to the laxity that prevails today, when the *Washington Post*, absolutely unhindered by the government, prints op-ed submissions by the likes of Mahmoud al-Zahar, a founder and top official of Hamas, which is a U.S.-designated terrorist organization, and Mousa Abu Marzook, a Hamas terrorist who is listed as a specially designated terrorist by the U.S. Treasury Department. [12] Similarly, a website run by the *Washington Post* and *Newsweek* saw fit to run a piece on the meaning of jihad written by Muhammad Hussein Fadlallah, a spiritual leader of Hezbollah, another U.S.-designated terrorist organization.[13] U.S. intelligence agents have suspected Fadlallah of helping to organize Hezbollah's 1983 suicide bombing attack on the Marine barracks in Beirut that killed 241 U.S. servicemen.[14]

It is hard to imagine the population on the home front during World War II waking up one morning, opening the paper, and finding a direct appeal to the American people from a top official from Nazi Germany's Propaganda Ministry, or an entreaty from an Imperial Japanese pilot suspected of participating in the attack on Pearl Harbor. And yet, ignoring the unarguable success of censorship policies in maintaining morale and protecting state secrets throughout the long days of World War II, liberals and libertarians incessantly bemoan the few, common-sense restrictions on civil liberties that the government has taken since September 11, denouncing them as abhorrent measures ushering in a totalitarian state.

The *New York Times*, naturally, led the charge, deploring parts of the Patriot Act for providing "license for federal agents to spy on innocent people and suppress dissent."[15] Tellingly, the paper declined to specify exactly whose right to dissent is being squelched. Joe Conason added this dire warning: "In America, where traditions of free expression and government accountability remain strong, such centralized power over the means of expression cannot easily be achieved—not even in wartime. Yet that difficulty hasn't discouraged the Republican regime from seeking *unprecedented* power over what we can see, hear, and read about our rulers and their policies" (emphasis added).[16]

To the contrary, the "Republican regime" did not seek out anything even remotely approaching the kind of censorship power that Roosevelt exerted during World War II. What's more, Roosevelt's policies themselves were hardly unprecedented. Those *New York Times* editors who see the Patriot Act as a powerful weapon against dissent should compare the act's actual stipulations to the kind of restrictions that President Wilson enacted during World War I. The section of the Patriot Act that the *Times* most vociferously attacked was the now-revoked stipulation permitting the government to access the library records of terrorism suspects. And indeed, allowing FBI agents to ascertain which books a terrorism suspect checked out did represent a new wartime restriction on civil liberties. But let's compare this authority to the kinds of powers claimed by the government during World War I. As Jonah Goldberg relates,

> Even as the government was churning out propaganda, it was silencing dissent. Wilson's Sedition Act banned "uttering, printing, writing, or publishing any disloyal, profane, scurrilous, or abusive language about the United States government or the military." The postmaster general was given the authority to deny mailing privileges to any publication he saw fit—effectively shutting it down. At least seventy-five periodicals were banned. Foreign publications were not allowed unless their content was first translated and approved by censors. Journalists also faced the very real threat of being jailed or having their supply of newsprint terminated by the War Industries Board.[17]

These policies were not dissimilar from those that had been adopted by President Lincoln. During the Civil War, not only were all telegraph messages subject to censorship, but the government also shut down dozens of newspapers and imprisoned their editors. Thousands of people were arrested for "disloyalty." Most famously, Lincoln suspended habeas corpus, allowing for the temporary abolition of normal legal procedures for suspected criminals.[18]

This is not to defend every wartime restriction approved by American presidents, or to imply that all these policies are needed today. I relate this history to make the point that in America's past, it was well understood by people of all political persuasions that in periods of wartime, when the nation faces a heightened national security threat, the government can and should exert certain powers that are not exercised during peacetime. As a trio of liberal advisors opined to the Roosevelt Administration in a communication justifying the evacuation of ethnic Japanese from the West Coast, "In time of national peril any reasonable doubt must be resolved in favor of action to preserve the national safety, not for the purpose of punishing those whose liberty may be temporarily affected by such action, but for the purpose of protecting the freedom of the nation which may be long impaired, if not permanently lost, by non-action."[19]

THE MEDIA'S ENDANGERMENT OF AMERICA

In order to help prosecute the current war on Islamic fascists, we need some small, reasonable restrictions on the media. This should not, by any means, impinge on any media outlet's ability to editorialize for or against the war; most of the mainstream media have lined up against the war in Iraq, and opposed nearly all of President Bush's national security policies. That is their right. But there is no reason why newspapers should remain free to publish direct appeals to the American public from members of designated terrorist organizations. Likewise, misguided activists like former President Jimmy Carter, who ignored warnings from the State Department and met with the Hamas leadership in Syria in an attempt to supplant the government's diplomatic program with his own, should be held to account by having his passport revoked—at a minimum.

Most important, the media should not enjoy the unfettered right to publish national security, intelligence, and military secrets. These revelations can be so damaging to national security that sanctions should be enforced not just against government officials who leak secrets, but also against the journalists and media outlets that disclose them. Currently, this remains a grey area in the law, with various court precedents protecting the media's right to publish secrets, while others have affirmed the government's right to forbid the publication of classified information if it would cause "grave and irreparable" danger.

This kind of danger was certainly caused by the *New York Times'* 2005 revelation of the National Security Agency's terrorist surveillance program. This secret program, a key tool in the war against Islamic terrorism, monitored communications between U.S.-based terrorism suspects and their foreign contacts. Although a judge later ruled the program illegal because the government did not seek warrants from the Foreign Intelligence Surveillance Act (FISA) courts for its wiretaps, that decision was later overturned. Nevertheless, in the meantime the government began petitioning for warrants to the FISA court, which proceeded to proclaim jurisdiction over the surveillance of foreign-based terrorism suspects merely if they used American communications networks.

Congress countered the FISA court's power grab by approving most elements of the original terrorist surveillance program. But this provided little solace to National Security Agency agents, whose surveillance efforts had been compromised by the leak to the *New*

York Times. Once terrorists know they're being monitored—and even *how* they're being monitored—the effectiveness of the surveillance is severely degraded.

Critics falsely claimed that the terrorist surveillance program was illegal. As lawyer David Rivkin notes, the president is vested with the constitutional authority to order electronic surveillance of both domestic- and foreign-based enemies during wartime.[20] But even if the program had been illegal, this would still not justify the revelation of its existence in the press. The U.S. already has firm procedures—codified in the Intelligence Community Whistleblower Protection Act of 1998—for whistleblowers to bring acts of malfeasance involving intelligence matters to Congress's attention. It is illegal for intelligence agents to leak this information to the press, and it should be illegal for the press to reveal it to the public.

Barack Obama surprised and disappointed a lot of his supporters in 2008 when he voted in favor of a FISA reform bill that provided retroactive immunity to telecom companies that were sued for cooperating with the terrorist surveillance program. While he deserves credit for voting to quash these politically motivated lawsuits, the depth of Obama's conviction is questionable, to say the least. His vote came shortly after he became the presumptive Democratic nominee in the presidential election, at a time when he was moving to the center on many issues. Until just weeks before his FISA vote, Obama had proudly worked with other Democrats to block immunity for telecom companies, threatening to filibuster any bill that included the measure. He declared, "I am proud to stand with Senator Dodd, Senator Feingold and a grassroots movement of Americans who are refusing to let President Bush put protections for special interests ahead of our security and our liberty. There is no reason why telephone companies should be given blanket immunity to cover violations of the rights of the

American people."[21] And soon after, Obama voted to do precisely that.

The fecklessness of politicians on this issue, and their focus on imaginary violations of civil liberties instead of the real scandal of media complicity in disclosing national secrets, has allowed this unacceptable situation to continue. Having faced no legal consequences for revealing the terrorist surveillance program, the *New York Times* was emboldened to repeat its shameful performance. In 2006, the *Times* and other newspapers published details of another secret anti-terrorism surveillance program, this one aimed at monitoring terrorism suspects' international banking transactions. President Bush denounced the program's disclosure as "disgraceful," declaring, "We're at war with a bunch of people who want to hurt the United States of America, and for people to leak that program, and for a newspaper to publish it, does great harm to the United States of America."[22]

Republican Congressman Peter T. King of New York called for the prosecution of the *Times* for treason, but the Justice Department declined to press charges. Thus, the president was left impotent as the media undermined another key tool for fighting terrorists.

It's clear that appeals to the media's sense of patriotism will fall on deaf ears. During the Bush years, the media blissfully endangered America's safety for the pleasure of striking a blow at a president they despised. The administration had asked the *Times* not to disclose the banking surveillance program, explaining how its revelation would damage national security. But *Times* editors imperiously dismissed the administration's concerns, arguing without any factual basis that terrorist financiers already knew their transactions were being monitored. In defending the paper's actions, *Times* executive editor Bill Keller did not make any specific allegations of illegality or impropriety against the program, instead citing the "discomfort" over its legality and oversight allegedly felt by "some" anonymous "officials." Keller also trumpeted the *Times*'s role as a government watchdog, proclaiming that "the people who invented this country saw an aggressive, independent press as a protective measure against the abuse of power in a democracy, and an essential ingredient for self-government."[23]

As a matter of general principle, that is true enough. But I have yet to find a statement from any of the Founding Fathers defending the press's right to publish state secrets during wartime. It was only because the Bush administration was so much less authoritarian than the administration of Abraham Lincoln or Woodrow Wilson or Franklin Delano Roosevelt that the *Times*'s right to publish was permitted to trump national security concerns. The Bush administration should have responded to the *New York Times*'s gross irresponsibility by prosecuting journalists, editors, and publishers who endanger the public by revealing secret anti-terrorism programs. As then White House press secretary Tony Snow remarked at the time, "The *New York Times* and other news organizations ought to think long and hard about whether a public's right to know, in some cases, might overwrite somebody's right to live."[24]

Even when there's absolutely no allegation of wrongdoing, it seems that many newspapers today take a perverse pride in revealing U.S. intelligence secrets. In December 2007, the *L.A. Times* revealed the existence of a secret CIA program to entice officials working on Iran's nuclear program to defect. The paper, citing anonymous current and former U.S. intelligence officials, described the effort as "part of a major intelligence push against Iran" designed to gain a more accurate understanding of Iran's nuclear activities and to hinder Iranian efforts to develop a nuclear weapon.

What possible justification exists for allowing the *L.A. Times* to sabotage a vital intelligence program against one of the world's top sponsors of international terrorism? Iran's nuclear development program is one of the most dangerous foreign policy challenges that we face today. Secret operations to subvert or impede Iran's development of nuclear weapons make the world a safer place and lessen the chances of war and nuclear terrorism. Yet, for the *L.A. Times*, considerations of national security take a back seat to the glory gained from publishing a big scoop.

This problem is not confined to newspapers. Yet another damaging leak occurred in October 2007, when the ABC News website posted clips from a new al Qaeda video featuring Osama bin Laden. It turns out that the U.S. government had penetrated the al Qaeda Internet communications system, known as Obelisk, and gotten hold of the video before al Qaeda had released it to the public. However, someone leaked the video to ABC News, whose Internet broadcast of the video tipped off al Qaeda that its communications system had been compromised. Unsurprisingly, al Qaeda then shut down the entire network. Rita Katz, the head of an intelligence group that helps the government monitor terrorist communications on the Internet, explained the consequences: "The government leak damaged our investigation into Al Qaeda's network. Techniques and sources that took years to develop became ineffective. As a result of the leak Al Qaeda changed their methods." A U.S. intelligence official added, "We saw the whole thing [Obelisk] shut down because of this leak.... We lost an important keyhole into the enemy."[25]

Nearly all mainstream newspapers have been scathing toward the Bush Administration for the intelligence failures surrounding Iraq's weapons of mass destruction program. But how can they demand that the U.S. improve its intelligence capabilities when the papers themselves actively undermine them? Tipping off international terrorists that their communications are being monitored, and informing hostile regimes that their officials are targeted as potential defectors, undermines national security while serving no public purpose whatsoever.

THE EXCEPTION THAT CONFIRMS THE RULE

Interestingly, among the numerous national security leaks since September 11, the only time liberals really became indignant was when conservative reporter Robert Novak seemed to out Valerie Plame as a CIA agent. Plame was married to former State Department official Joe Wilson, who became a darling of the left when he published op-eds in the *New York Times* casting doubt on the veracity of some of the Bush Administration's claims regarding Iraqi efforts to develop weapons of mass destruction. In an editorial on the case, the *New York Times* stated its opposition to leak investigations "in principle," and also warned against prosecuting Novak or any other journalist. This, of course, could have set a worrisome precedent for the paper. Nevertheless, the *Times* declared that some leaks are morally "wrong," and then speculated—incorrectly—that the White House had leaked Plame's identity as a CIA agent to Novak, an act which it characterized as "a serious assault on free speech and an egregious abuse of power."

But is it any less of an abuse of power for the *Times* to compromise national security by betraying the details of secret intelligence programs for monitoring terrorist suspects? A person cannot honestly support some national security leaks and condemn others, depending on the perceived political agenda of the leaker. (The *Times*, unsurprisingly, became much less concerned by the ramifications of the Plame leak when it was revealed that the leak had not come from the White House, but rather from then deputy secretary of state Richard Armitage, a man not known to have close ties to President Bush.)

The Plame leak, in fact, does not seem to have damaged national security, as apparently Plame no longer had covert status when the Novak column appeared (this according to, among others, a former CIA covert agent who had been her supervisor).[26] But if she *had* been an active secret agent, and if Novak had known that, then, as I argued in a column at the time, charges should have been brought against the leaker, Novak himself, and every publisher who ran his column, just as the *New York Times* and *L.A. Times* should have been held responsible for publishing details of secret intelligence activities.

The hypocrisy of liberals on this issue is astounding. On the left, there was an incredible outcry over the outing of Plame, with all kinds of demands for prosecution of the leakers solely because the "victims" of the leak—Valerie Plame and Joe Wilson—were stridently opposed to President Bush and the Iraq War. Predictably, however, liberals exhibited no such concern in June 2008 when the *New York Times* published the name of the CIA interrogator who questioned Khalid Sheikh Mohammed, the architect of the September 11 attacks. The CIA pleaded in vain with the *Times* not to name the interrogator (who the *Times* acknowledged had not waterboarded Mohammed or used any other harsh interrogation techniques), arguing that the publicity would put him and his family in physical danger. The *Times* defended publishing the interrogator's name as necessary for the credibility of the story. They asserted this even while acknowledging that another former CIA interrogator who had been exposed by the media had been bombarded with death threats, fired from his job (as a security risk), and had, at least temporarily, to flee to Mexico with his family to go into hiding.[27]

In June 2006 the House of Representatives passed a resolution, opposed by most Democrats, condemning the media's disclosure of secret anti-terror programs. The bill declared that the House "expects the cooperation of all news media organizations" to protect the government's capability "to identify, disrupt, and capture terrorists." In our current war, however, the media has proven that it would rather help our enemies than help protect the lives of Americans. Perhaps the media will be more circumspect now that its own preferred candidate has been elected. But we can't afford to take any more chances. Congress must clarify the law so that publishing government secrets that endanger our national security and our wartime efforts will be severely punished.

Approving laws to defend national secrets would not impact the right to protest the war or any other government policy. To the contrary, we must zealously guard the right to dissent. Long may Americans stand on our hind legs and shout our outrage and opposition to and at our government. We may be polite or rude. We may be thoughtful or we may scream insults. Either way, a healthy democracy requires a wide berth for protest.

As a newspaperman myself, I fully appreciate the indispensable role that the media play in a free society. However, if publishers and editors won't exert a modicum of self-restraint when it comes to national security, then the government must invoke the force of law to compel them to behave responsibly. American newspapers should foster a free debate on government policies, not act as agents of enemy sabotage.[28]

CHAPTER 6

★　　★　　★

A LAW CODE
FOR WARTIME

IT IS UNACCEPTABLE THAT THE LEGAL SYSTEM TODAY IS ENFEEBLING THE war against Islamic terror. Too much emphasis has been placed on the legal process as an end in itself. What is ignored is that the law has a higher purpose: to strengthen a country through the wise resolution of disputes. But when the legal system undercuts national security and makes the population more vulnerable to terrorism, it is simply dysfunctional.

In our present war we've witnessed a relentless campaign by liberals and libertarians to constrain executive power to a level much lower than it traditionally has been in wartime. This effort must be resisted at all costs by any president—whether Republican or Democrat. Barack Obama was a harsh critic of executive power under President Bush, but that doesn't mean he'll keep that position when he assumes office. In fact, there's reason to hope that as president he'll come to the same realization as Franklin Roosevelt did: that the awesome responsibility of leading our nation in war requires a president to assume the enhanced powers needed to bring victory.

ENEMY COMBATANTS

Imagine if during World War II every captured enemy soldier had been entitled to a trial in a U.S. criminal court. They would have been provided with lawyers and enjoyed the presumption of innocence. During discovery, the government would have had to turn over to the defendants' lawyers all the information and intelligence they had collected against them, even if it meant revealing secret intelligence sources buried within opposing militaries or governments, or identifying partisans living in occupied territories. Their lawyers would have argued that the soldiers had been involuntarily impressed into service or that they had never actually done any fighting. Prosecutors would have had the burden of proving beyond a reasonable doubt that the soldiers, in fact, had actively conspired to harm the United States or U.S. citizens.

It's hard to believe the American people would have countenanced these rights being extended to enemy combatants. How would honoring these rights, which our enemies did not extend to our own troops, have contributed to victory? Clearly, it would have had the opposite effect—not only would the courts have freed enemy soldiers to fight another day, but our soldiers would have been hamstrung on the battlefield, being forced to catalogue carefully all the circumstances under which every enemy soldier was captured, and to follow a maze of legal procedures to ensure courts would not throw out their captures on some technicality.

Yet, this is similar to the situation in which we found ourselves throughout the 1990s, when captured terrorists within our own borders were processed by the criminal justice system instead of being handled by the military as national security threats. The second terrorist attack on the World Trade Center, on September 11, 2001, finally provoked some government initiatives to detain, classify, and prosecute captured terrorists in a way that no longer undermines our national security. However, refusing to learn from the past, "human rights advocates" are forcing us to return to the failed legal model of the Clinton era.

Bewailing the supposed injustice of trying captured terrorists before military tribunals, liberal activists have struggled relentlessly to confer on captured terrorists all the legal rights of U.S. citizens. And because, as in World War II, Congress, the president, and the American people have all expressed support for keeping enemy combatants outside the criminal justice system, activists have resorted to an end-run around legal authority and public opinion by using their customary method—legislating their policies through the courts.

Again, to get some perspective on the current debate, it's instructive to recall the kinds of homeland security policies the United States adopted during previous wars. During World War II, in order to safeguard the West Coast from Japanese espionage and attack, President Franklin Roosevelt signed Executive Order 9066, which formed the basis of the government's evacuation and eventual internment of ethnic Japanese residents. While the fate of the Japanese evacuees is well known, the restrictions placed on residents of Hawaii, with its sizeable ethnic Japanese population, have largely been forgotten. As Michelle Malkin recounts in her book *In Defense of Internment*, the government placed all of Hawaii under martial law, enabling it to undertake extraordinary measures to fight subversion:

> Mail and newspapers were censored. Phone calls were monitored. Liquor sales were banned. Every civilian over the age of six was registered, fingerprinted, and required to carry

identification at all times. Americans of German, Italian, or Japanese ancestry were prohibited from assembling in groups, and from owning firearms, cameras, and radio receivers. The writ of habeas corpus was suspended, and hundreds of U.S. citizens considered potentially subversive, almost all of them Nisei, were confined without trial.[1]

Note that these policies applied to *U.S. citizens*. The powers exercised by the Bush Administration after September 11 against enemy combatants did not even remotely approach the kind of severe infringements on civil liberties routinely approved on the home front by the liberal hero, President Roosevelt. To the contrary, President Bush's most insistent reaction to September 11 was to insist that Islam is an inherently peaceful religion that is being perverted by a tiny minority of misguided extremists. Far from rounding up American Muslims into internment camps, the government refused even to allow common-sense profiling of Arabs and Muslims at airports—this after nineteen Muslim Arab hijackers slaughtered 3,000 Americans.

Yet, liberals today are forcing us to give more rights to captured terrorists than were granted to many U.S. citizens during past wars. The focus of their complaints has been the detainees held at Guantanamo Bay. Liberals and libertarians argue that these prisoners should be classified as civilians, be granted lawyers, and have their cases moved from the military to the criminal court system. While liberal and libertarian activists portray the Gitmo detainees as victims of some new, insidious legal convention, it is the activists themselves who are demanding a completely new legal framework. In U.S. history, we have never provided lawyers to enemy combatants. The Law of Armed Conflict as well as the Geneva Conventions provide for the detention of enemy combatants until the end of hostilities. That is what we've always done, and that's what we did under the Bush administration.

Some detainees, however, such as September 11 mastermind Khalid Sheikh Mohammed, were to be tried by a military commission as stipulated by the Military Commissions Act. This legislation, passed by Congress and signed by President Bush in 2006, provided a vital corrective to the Supreme Court's *Hamdan* v. *Rumsfeld* decision, in which the court banned the previous system of military commissions authorized by President Bush. In the *Hamdan* decision, indicative in so many ways of the limitless judicial overreach of liberal judges, the court trampled upon the president's traditional authority as commander in chief, including his power to convene military commissions, as well as the authority of military commanders to prosecute war. As Justice Clarence Thomas noted in his blistering dissent, "The plurality's willingness to second-guess the Executive's judgments in this context, based upon little more than its unsupported assertions, constitutes an unprecedented departure from the traditionally limited role of the courts with respect to war and an unwarranted intrusion on executive authority."[2]

But the courts felt provoked when the legislative and executive branches reasserted their authority by passing the Military Commissions Act; our imperial judiciary was determined to establish its wartime domination of both Congress and the presidency. In June 2008 the Supreme Court ruled 5–4 in *Boumediene* v. *Bush* that alien enemy combatants held at Guantanamo Bay have the right to challenge their captivity in a civilian court. This decision, an egregious violation of the separation of powers, extends "rights" unprecedented in U.S. history to enemy combatants, thus guaranteeing that the courts will be clogged up for years with frivolous appeals citing every conceivable technicality as a reason to release captured jihadists. And it is beyond dispute that some terrorists will be let go while others will not be imprisoned in the first place if the circumstances of their capture don't meet whatever arbitrary standards the courts decree. Justice Antonin Scalia's dissent succinctly related the consequences of the decision: America is "at war with radical Islamists," he affirmed, and the court's verdict "will make the war harder on us. It will almost certainly cause more Americans to be killed."[3]

With all the publicity over the detention center at Guantanamo Bay, it may surprise a lot of people to discover that we hold fewer than 300 prisoners there. At its peak Gitmo housed around 800, but most have been transferred to their home countries or released as a result of tribunal hearings—in which they're entitled to challenge their designation as enemy combatants—or annual status hearings before an Administrative Review Board. If the prison system at Guantanomo Bay is so unjust and oppressive, how is it that through its own processes it has released or repatriated nearly two-thirds of its detainees in the first few years of its operation?

One thing is certain: for the foreseeable future, we will endure an unending parade of legal actions, supported by a wide variety of leftwing and "civil liberties" interest groups, challenging every aspect of the detention regime for terrorism suspects. Ignoring the long history of wartime restrictions in America, litigants will continue to decry the "unprecedented" infringement of these jihadists' civil rights. Because even the Democrat-controlled Congress has shown no intention of stripping the president of his authority as commander in chief, the courts are the activists' only route to undermine executive branch powers. It is an effort to litigate the war on Islamic fascism out of existence.

The criminal justice system simply is not designed to handle terrorism cases and enemy combatants. Among other problems, criminal trials for terrorism suspects pose a serious threat to national security. In such trials, the government must provide defendants with reams of sensitive intelligence information related to the case. These can easily compromise informants and active operations. In *Willful Blindness*, Andy McCarthy, the prosecutor of the jihadist cell led by the "Blind Sheikh" Omar Abdel-Rahman that carried out the 1993 World Trade Center bombing, recounts the way in which Osama bin Laden discovered in 1995 that the U.S. government considered him a terrorism suspect: bin Laden was alerted when he received the list, on which his name appeared, of unindicted co-conspirators that McCarthy's prosecution team was required to provide to the defense during the Blind Sheik's trial.[4]

Although defendants cannot legally pass on classified information received from prosecutors during their trial, it is questionable, to say the least, whether al Qaeda suspects can be expected to observe these legal niceties. As McCarthy notes, "The congenial rules of access to attorneys, paralegals, investigators, and visitors make it a very simple matter for accused terrorists to transmit what they learn in discovery to their confederates—and we know that they do so."[5]

Even if it provokes domestic and international criticism, President Obama must continue to guard zealously executive branch prerogatives to prosecute war. This pertains not only to the processing of enemy combatants, but to interrogation techniques used against them as well. Of course, any outright abuses, such as those that occurred at Abu Ghraib, must be prosecuted to the fullest extent of the law—which they were. (If possible, however, such prosecutions should not be publicized, as such abuses are propaganda triumphs for the enemy.) But ambiguous issues, such as the use of waterboarding and stress positions, should be left to the discretion of the president, the military, and intelligence interrogators. The question of whether these techniques are consistent with the Geneva

Conventions should only be decided by the president, who has the constitutional right to interpret international treaties.

Legal challenges to presidential authority must be met head on and defeated. The path of least resistance for Obama would be simply to relinquish many of the president's wartime powers to the courts, allowing them to micromanage the war effort, with all the attending deleterious consequences. But allowing the courts to assume the mantle of commander in chief would be a disastrous alteration of the Constitution's careful system of checks and balances. By design, the president is privy to all kinds of foreign policy discussions, military data, terrorism assessments, and clandestine intelligence that the courts are not. This, along with the president's democratic mandate, puts him in a far better position to prosecute a war than are unelected judges. America's successful wartime presidents have always insisted on their constitutional right to lead wars unencumbered by judicial second-guessing.

President Obama must follow the same path, lest presidential power dissipate into the hands of others. His statements on issues of presidential power have not been encouraging, however. "We're going to close Guantanamo," he has declared, adding, "and we're going to restore habeas corpus.... We're going to lead by example, by not just word but by deed."[6] He also opposed the Military Commissions Act of 2006, repeatedly condemned the alleged "abuses" and "torture" of terror detainees during the Bush administration, and displayed stunning naïvete in citing the prosecution of the 1993 World Trade Center bombers as a good model for handling terrorism cases.[7]

But I have some hope for Obama. It's easy to criticize wartime leadership from the safe confines of a Senate seat, but it's something else entirely when 300 million people are depending on you personally to keep them safe. Even if he follows through with his misguided plan to withdraw quickly from Iraq, Obama will still have to face down the jihadist threat throughout the world as well as in the homeland.

Expectations among libertarians that Obama will release prisoners held at Guantanamo Bay, even if he shuts down the facility, are probably misplaced. As former general counsel of the 9/11 Commission, Democrat Daniel Marcus, observes, "It would be very difficult for a new president to come in and say, 'I don't believe what the C.I.A. is saying about these guys.'"[8] Indeed, hardly a week after Obama's election, his intelligence advisors began indicating that a radical overhaul of President Bush's intelligence policies was unlikely.[9] When actually forced to choose whether to put Americans at risk on his watch in order to provide more comfort to captured jihadists, Obama may surprise a lot of people—including his own supporters—by discovering the importance of presidential prerogatives he'd previously condemned.

THE CORROSIVE CULTURE OF POLITICAL CORRECTNESS

At this juncture, it's worth noting an obvious point: better laws won't make us any safer if they're not enforced. It's all well and good for the president and Congress to legislate new security measures, but they also need to exert the proper oversight to ensure that the federal bureaucracies actually enforce the laws as they are legally required to do.

A single example conveys the drastic—even deadly—consequences that can result when bureaucrats subordinate security measures to other concerns. The State Department is tasked with overseeing international consular offices responsible for issuing visas to foreigners. Applicants must fill out an application and provide personal information in order to be approved. The conditions an applicant must meet are quite high—the law states that U.S. officials must consider nearly all applicants as hopeful immigrants, and the burden of proof rests on the applicants to show that they intend to leave America before their visa expires. Thus, even a complete and accurate application should face some tough scrutiny.

And yet, in what seems to be a systemic problem in the State Department, some high-ranking officials have shown much more concern with currying favor with foreigners than with advocating American interests or even protecting American national security. After the September 11 attacks, reporter Joel Mowbray got hold of the application forms of fifteen of the nineteen hijackers. Mowbray showed the forms to six experts with experience in Consular Affairs. All six reached the same conclusion: the applications were so incomplete that all fifteen should have been rejected. Instead of providing an address where they'd be staying in America, most of the terrorists wrote vague locations such as "New York," "Hotel," or simply "No." And all were approved, opening up America's door to our enemies.[10]

As Mowbray discovered, the approval was part of a "courtesy culture" within the Consular Affairs bureaucracy that prioritized the convenience of foreign visa applicants over America's national security. Some of the hijackers were even approved through a "visa express" program that allowed Saudis to apply for visas through travel agencies, with only cursory reviews of their applications by U.S. consulates that typically did not include a personal interview.[11]

Thus we see that the law, in fact, should have been adequate to keep out most of the hijackers. But an unenforced law is no law at all. The president must ensure that laws are actually applied by maintaining accountability among the appointed leaderships of the various federal bureaucracies. This is especially important in any national security bureaucracy. Unfortunately, President Bush did not always insist on such accountability, tending instead to support subordinates who displayed loyalty, even when their performance proved inadequate. This problem is especially pressing in the area of immigration, where ludicrously insufficient enforcement measures have bred a deep disrespect for the law. The result is that a large swath of the Mexican border remains wide open to illegal immigrants, and there's a lax system for tracking down visa absconders. This has created an important security threat as millions of foreigners continue to take up residence in our country illegally.

In order to enforce our public security laws rigorously, we have to root out the corrosive culture of political correctness that has become ingrained throughout the government, including in our security services.

Concerns over political correctness have greatly diminished our security efforts, leading to a number of terrorist attacks that appear to have been preventable. Not only were the September 11 hijackers given visas due to concerns for political correctness, but the entire plot may well have been stopped in its tracks if the FBI had acted on the Phoenix memo, a communication written in July 2001 by an Arizona FBI agent calling for an investigation of the large number of suspicious Muslim and Arab men registered in U.S. flight schools. The urgent memo, however, was immediately buried in the FBI bureaucracy; in his testimony before the Senate Judiciary Committee, former FBI director Robert Mueller simply could not explain why no one acted upon such a vital warning.[12]

The 9/11 Commission downplayed the Phoenix memo. In a brief, three paragraph section on it, the commission's official report noted that the agent's warning was not moved up the chain of command, and then briskly speculated that it probably would not have led agents to uncover the September 11 plot. The report lamely asserted that "the warning system was not looking for information such as the July 2001 FBI report of potential terrorist interest in various kinds of aircraft training in Arizona."[13] It's not surprising that the commission would trivialize the Phoenix memo, because the memo brings up politically explosive questions about the culture of political correctness in our security services. In fact, the culture of political correctness is such a sensitive issue that the commission declined to mention it even once in its entire 400-plus page report.

And the Phoenix memo was not the first time that politically correct considerations hindered terrorism investigations. Similar tales abound in McCarthy's *Willful Blindness*. For example, McCarthy relates that the FBI had the Blind Sheikh's jihadist cell under surveillance on July 23, 1989, when FBI agents parked in a van were observing a group of sixteen jihadists taking target practice at a shooting range. Noticing the van, the jihadists pounded on it until an agent emerged. The jihadists began complaining that the feds were harassing and victimizing them because they were Muslims. As McCarthy recounts,

> "Islamophobia" had not yet come into vogue as a grievance-industry rally cry—that would be several years and several Islamic terror attacks later. But, as is reliably the case today, the posturing worked to a fare-thee-well. The Bureau and JTTF [Joint Terrorism Task Force] had been curious, and they had been right: Dangerous men were readying themselves to be more dangerous. They were highly worth monitoring. Nevertheless, they maintained their innocence with defiant confidence.... The FBI is sensitive to even the emptiest allegation that it has violated someone's civil rights. The [surveillance] effort was thus aborted since, as a practical matter, additional surveillance would have been much more

difficult now that the agents had been "made" by their sub-jects.[14]

Several jihadists present that day went on to bomb the World Trade Center less than four years later.

It's hard to eliminate a problem when you refuse to even acknowledge it—and I mean this in the most literal sense. In 2008, the Bush Administration advised various federal agencies, including the Department of Homeland Security and the National Counter Terrorism Center, to avoid describing Islamic terrorists with offensive-sounding terms such as "jihadists," "mujahedeen," or "Islamo-fascists." Instead, based on the recommendations of anonymous Muslims, it instructed officials to use vague formulations like "violent extremists" or simply "terrorists."[15] While there may be good reasons to change our government language patterns, it's crystal clear that political correctness—not shrewdness—is driving this policy.

The culture of political correctness continues today in our security services, beginning with their relentless pursuit of "diversity" in their hiring decisions. When FBI agents and Homeland Security officials are subjected to Muslim-sensitivity training sessions by CAIR, a radical Islamic advocacy group that was named as an unindicted co-conspirator in a terrorism financing trial, it becomes clear that our security agencies need to change dramatically their internal culture.[16]

The unremitting pressure that interest groups place on all our federal agencies to prioritize "diversity" and cultural sensitivity above any other value—including national security—represents a severe assault on America's internal security. Thankfully, it seems that the American people are starting to rebel against the diversity shtick. When a group of six Muslim imams, supported by CAIR, sued U.S.

Airways for removing them from a plane for acting suspiciously, the lawsuit met with widespread derision from the public, who referred to the litigants as "the flying imams." Observers rightly identified the most dangerous part of the suit—the imams' inclusion of unnamed passengers who had reported their suspicious activity to the airline. If the suit had succeeded, it would have forced airline security personnel to treat Muslims with *special* leniency or else risk being hauled into court for "Islamophobia." What's more, the general public would have had to give special consideration before reporting suspicious Muslims, knowing that they could be sued just for voicing their concerns.[17]

The flying imams case finally provoked a rare bit of government action to protect the public from political correctness run amuck— Congress passed a measure providing immunity from legal actions for transport passengers who report suspicious behavior to the authorities. In response to the immunity law, the imams dropped the anonymous tipsters from their lawsuit, although the airlines and airport police remain defendants in the flying imam lawsuit.

There should be no exception to security rules for the most culturally aggressive groups in America. As long as we face a unique terrorist threat from Muslim men, it is absolutely appropriate and necessary that they be subjected to additional security scrutiny. On the heels of the flying imam legislation already approved, Congress should pass a law making airlines and airport security personnel immune from lawsuits for security-based ethnic profiling.

Opponents of common sense ethnic profiling like Norman Mineta, the former Transportation Secretary who refused to institute ethnic profiling on airlines after September 11, are quick to draw spurious comparisons to the Japanese internment during World War II—as if there's no qualitative difference between searching someone's suitcase and forcing them into an internment camp.

Internment was an extreme measure, but during World War II, as in previous wars, the nation temporarily adopted tough—even unjust—policies in order to win the war. Today, security hawks such as myself ask not that any citizens be rounded up and interned based on their ethnicity, but rather that some endure security procedures that last a few minutes longer than for everyone else. Security concerns need to trump cultural sensitivity, as explained by Debra Burlingame, whose brother piloted the doomed Flight 77 on September 11: "To compel [flight attendants] to ignore all but the most unambiguous cases of suspicious behavior is to further enable terrorists who act in ways meant to defy easy categorization. As the American Airlines flight attendants who literally jumped on 'shoe bomber' Richard Reid demonstrated, cabin crews are sharply attuned to unusual or abnormal behavior and they must not be second-guessed, or hamstrung by misguided notions of political correctness."[18]

IN DEFENSE OF WESTERN LAW

America must not only fight aggressively against the threat of violence posed by Islamic terrorists, but we must also guard our way of life. This means, first and foremost, that we must defend our legal code, based on Judeo-Christian values as well as centuries of European legal precedent and intellectual thought, from the intrusions of Sharia law.

The biggest threats we face today from proponents of Sharia law are the various maneuvers through which they are attempting to ban criticism or even satire of Islam, and prohibit discussion of Islamic terrorism networks. Until recently, the most successful attempt at this form of censorship was through "libel tourism," a scheme in which wealthy Saudis file lawsuits in British courts against book authors or publishers from America and other countries. Because English libel law places the burden of proof on the defendant, it's relatively easy for litigants to get favorable judgments, which are then used to intimidate other authors and publishers.

The template was set by Saudi plutocrat Khalid bin Mahfouz, who since 2002 has repeatedly filed lawsuits in England against authors, including Americans, who have written about Mahfouz's alleged financial ties to terrorist groups like al Qaeda. Having successfully silenced dozens of authors since 2002, bin Mahfouz achieved his most infamous "victory" when he intimidated Cambridge University Press into suppressing completely a book by two American authors, *Alms for Jihad*, which explored how jihadists fund terrorism through the auspices of Islamic charities. In an unusually obsequious settlement, the publisher agreed to pay bin Mahfouz damages, pulp all unsold copies of the book, and request that libraries pull the book from their shelves. U.S. Congressman Frank Wolf referred to the settlement as "basically a book burning," warning correctly of its chilling effect against other authors.[19]

The phenomenon of libel tourism posed a real threat to American authors seeking to expose terrorism networks and their financiers. The fact that the whole exercise was run through foreign courts presented an unacceptable infringement of American sovereignty. Thankfully, this situation has been partially resolved. In 2004, bin Mahfouz sued New York-based author Rachel Ehrenfeld for discussing him in her book, *Funding Evil: How Terrorism is Financed—and How to Stop It*. A British court ordered Ehrenfeld to pay bin Mahfouz $225,900, publicly apologize to him, and destroy the book. In response, New York governor David Paterson signed legislation providing broad protection for New York publishers and authors against libel tourism. As Paterson noted, the law quickly needs to be followed up by federal legislation that would protect authors in all fifty states from this kind of legal jihad.[20]

America needs to learn a lesson about the legal jihad from the example of many of our Western allies. A cautionary tale can be gleaned in Canada, where quasi-judicial "human rights commissions" have assumed the authority to dictate what statements, writings, and ideas are too intolerant to be allowed. For a number of years, self-styled human rights crusaders have filed complaints with the commissions against sundry crackpots and fringe racists for allegedly inciting hatred through inflammatory speech or writings. It was only a matter of time before Islamic activists got into the act. In 2006, Canadian Muslim activists filed complaints with human rights commissions against Ezra Levant for publishing the Danish Mohammed cartoons in his magazine, the *Western Standard*. Shortly thereafter, other Muslim activists filed complaints against Canadian news magazine *Maclean's* when it published an excerpt from Mark Steyn's book, *America Alone*, which argues that Europe will likely become culturally Islamic in the future due to the demographic growth and cultural assertiveness of Europe's Muslims.

The commissions eventually dismissed these complaints, but the fact that Levant and *Maclean's* were put through the judicial ringer in the first place is an outrage to Western legal traditions. The lesson to be learned here is that "tolerance," "diversity," and "multiculturalism" are not values that should receive legal protection, because such laws will inevitably be abused by the most culturally assertive minority groups to silence their critics. The kinds of enhanced censorship policies that I advocated for wartime in the previous chapter must be designed to serve the national interest, and today the primary national interest is the defeat of Islamic terrorism. Using "tolerance" as a rhetorical bludgeon to stifle criticism, analysis, or even mockery of our enemies—or the religion that motivates them—does not further the cause of victory in our current war. To the contrary, it hinders our efforts, and is therefore unacceptable. Legally infringing on free speech and free thought in the name of tolerance is hardly a rational objective for any American constitutionalist—libertarian or otherwise.

Additionally, as a society, we must be vigilant against the cultural accommodation of Islam in America. We've seen escalating demands for Islamic cultural exceptions in recent years, such as refusals by Islamic cab drivers to accept passengers who carry alcohol or are accompanied by guide dogs; the refusal of Muslim cashiers to handle pork products; the institution of gender segregation in multi-faith prayer rooms at American universities, and the installation of footbaths in universities to accommodate Islamic prayer rituals; and the enforcement of gender segregation during certain hours at a gym at Harvard University.[21]

The experience of many Western nations clearly shows that these kinds of accommodations, far from bringing about multicultural harmony, simply provoke more intrusive demands. What's most worrying is that the toleration of the expression of foreign values inevitably leads to demands to codify them in law.

The best example of this process is found in Britain, where the public accommodation of Islamic values has led to the establishment of a parallel Islamic legal system. Unofficial Sharia courts have sprung up throughout Britain, adjudicating everything from divorce settlements to violent crimes within Muslim communities. This accommodation of Islamic law is praised by some as a tolerant dose of "legal pluralism." Such advocates, swept up in the excitement of multicultural tolerance, seem unfazed by the unsavory tenets of Islamic law that the courts enforce. According to a *Daily Mail* investigation of the Sharia courts, "[Women] are excluded from hearing cases, and sexual crimes against them are rarely heard because if a daughter is raped, it is often considered best for the family to keep quiet about it. Under Sharia law, a raped woman brings 'aayib,' or shame, to the family because losing virginity out of wedlock (under whatever circumstances) is one of the gravest sins in Islam."[22]

The longer these courts have operated, the more demands Britain has faced to give them official sanction. Indeed, as long as they're allowed to function anyway, the British government doesn't seem to have much of a logical argument for *not* recognizing them. According to the *Daily Telegraph*, "Extremists were said to have used the spread of Sharia courts to justify calls for Islamic law to be adopted 'wholesale' for Muslims living in Britain." But an earlier *Telegraph* article revealed that these demands are already being voiced by more than just an extremist fringe—the paper reported that Faizul Aqtab Siddiqi, a barrister and principal of an Islamic college, "predicted that there would be a formal network of Muslim courts within a decade."[23]

And Siddiqi's prediction looks like a safe bet. In September 2008, the *Sunday Times* reported that the British government has "quietly" vested numerous Sharia courts with official power to rule on a range of cases—including, most disturbingly, cases of domestic violence.[24] This outcome was sadly inevitable once the door was opened by allowing Sharia law to make inroads into British law in the first place.

This alternative legal system has spread in Britain alongside a parallel, Sharia-compliant banking system that has been encouraged by the British government.[25] The willing diminution of some of the pillars of Western culture in Britain—the legal and financial systems—in favor of Sharia law is a stunning development that I predicted in my previous book. It demonstrates how an aggressive minority comprising just 3 percent of the population can quickly erode societal unity. In February 2008, the Archbishop of

Canterbury provoked outrage when he proclaimed that the adoption of aspects of Sharia law in the UK "seemed unavoidable." While I do not share the archbishop's sanguine view of the benefits of Sharia law, it's hard to argue that his prediction of Britain's future trajectory was not 100 percent accurate.

And Anglicans are not alone in welcoming Sharia law to Britain. In May 2008, Canon Gerard Tartaglia, priest of the Catholic Archdiocese of Glasgow, related his serene thoughts on the introduction of Islamic law in the UK: "It is inevitable there will be influence from Islamic law to one degree or another. I cannot see how it can be avoided, but nor can I imagine our society adopting laws which would not be of benefit. And it may be that the legislators introduce elements of Islamic law and that we will be none the wiser."[26]

Advocates of cultural accommodation to Islam don't appear concerned by the question of whether a population can retain any sense of national unity when it is Balkanized into various religious sects subject to different sets of laws. A nation should be comprised of one people subject to one legal code—until relatively recently, very few Westerners would have argued otherwise. America should learn from the mistakes of its Western allies and studiously avoid any steps toward the slippery slope of legal apartheid.

A law code should both reflect and positively influence the national character of the people it governs. This means, above all, that there should be no legal exceptions for foreign customs and values. If we hope to remain "one nation under God," we must continue to insist on rigid adherence to a single law code, carefully crafted to further the preservation and perpetuation of the American nation.[27]

★   ★   ★

CHAPTER 7

PUTTING AMERICA'S INTERESTS FIRST

"DO NOT LET SPACIOUS PLANS FOR A NEW WORLD DIVERT YOUR energies from saving what is left of the old." So said Winston Churchill. The great wartime leader was issuing instructions for improving British housing damaged in World War II, but his comment represents wise advice for American diplomats and policy makers, who are too focused today on grand ideological schemes for changing the world. The more they focus on the bright, shining future they think their policies will create, the more they lose sight of the needs and demands of the present moment. If we want a more successful foreign policy, we should begin by acknowledging that foreign policy should not function as a means fundamentally to change the world.

Because America has no single national interest, we shouldn't base our foreign policy on any one ideological goal, whether spreading democracy, securing world peace, or maintaining international stability. Instead, we should adopt a course I would call "pragmatic

internationalism." This policy would be based on a constant monitoring and practical assessment of the American national interest.
Rejecting isolationism outright, the United States should seek to
maintain and strengthen its position of leadership in the world,
without fearing to resort to military action whenever necessary. But
we must acknowledge our inherent limitations; even as the world's
lone superpower, America cannot fashion a brand new world out of
the one we now inhabit.

Downgrading ideology in favor of pragmatic internationalism
also means we must be careful not to over-emphasize lessons from
the past. While it may be true that those who don't learn from the
past are doomed to repeat it, we can't turn any single historical lesson into an ideological dogma that we apply in every scenario. The
best example of this is the ritual invocation of the Munich Agreement that helped pave the way to World War II. British prime minister Neville Chamberlin's consent to feeding Czechoslovakia to the
Nazis has rightly gone down in history as a disastrous act of
appeasement that only whetted the appetite of a murderous, expansionist Germany. But the frequently applied lesson from this
episode—that appeasement will always backfire and stoke aggression—is not true in every situation. In fact, if you look at British
policy from the time of Oliver Cromwell up through the twentieth
century, you'll see that Britain regularly "appeased" various tinpot
dictators all over the world as it successfully maintained and
expanded its empire. The key consideration for British policy makers was not whether any given policy was an act of appeasement,
but whether the policy furthered the empire's interests.

The main schools of foreign policy thinking today—especially
neo-conservatism and liberalism—put forward overly-ambitious,
ideological goals that the United States lacks the means to achieve.
They spread our limited resources too thinly in attempts to improve

the world in remote places that are of little consequence to U.S. national security. Here's what's wrong with the various foreign policy outlooks today:

NEO-CONSERVATISM

Neo-conservatism is exhibit A of the perils of an ideological foreign policy. For neo-conservatives, foreign policy is premised on an unshakeable belief in the righteousness of spreading democracy. Despite their mistakes, however, it should be said up front that neo-conservatives are on solid ground in arguing for the benefits of democracy. There's no doubt that the world would be much safer if tyrannies gave way to democracies, since democracies rarely go to war with each other. As the leader of the free world, it's naturally in America's interests for democracy to spread at the expense of the sundry dictatorships, kleptocracies, and communist holdovers that largely comprise our enemies.

But neo-conservatives take this ideology to an impractical extreme. Instead of acknowledging that the goal of any foreign policy is to serve America's interests, and viewing democratization as a means to achieve that goal, they have made democratization a goal in itself—not only a goal, but *the primary* goal of U.S. foreign policy. As a result, we've suffered a string of foreign policy setbacks that the neo-cons dubiously present as "progress" toward the utopian ideal of worldwide self-government.

For example, we cannot, in any conceivable way, consider the election of Islamic fundamentalists to power in the Middle East as something that benefits America's interests. Yet this was exactly the result we got when American pressure for the democratization of the Palestinian Authority led to the terrorist group Hamas winning the Palestinian parliamentary elections. When we have an anti-American band of Islamic fundamentalists gaining power in a key geopolitical area, it shouldn't make us feel any better that it was democratically elected. And forcing democracy in other key countries like Egypt, where U.S. pressure resulted in local elections dominated by the fundamentalists of the Muslim Brotherhood, would likely have a similar outcome.

These criticisms do not imply that we should strip our foreign policy of all its ideological considerations. America has traditionally presented its foreign policy in moral terms. This stems from a certain feature of the American character that has always sought to fight its wars in the name of a moral cause, which we usually do. John McCain captured this spirit during his 2008 presidential campaign when he declared, after being asked to name America's greatest moral failure, "Throughout our existence, perhaps we have not devoted ourselves to causes greater than our self-interest."[1] So giving our foreign policy a moral tone by paying tribute to democracy, freedom, and human rights will always be necessary, and we shouldn't forget that, as a general rule, the world becomes safer as democracy spreads.

But neo-conservatives tend to get swept up in their own moralizing to the point that their arguments cross over into emotional propaganda. This seems to have been what happened with President George W. Bush who, after the September 11 attacks, embraced the cause of spreading democracy with the zeal of a convert. If one looks back at Bush's second inaugural address, delivered in January 2005, the president outstripped even Woodrow Wilson in his unmitigated passion for opposing international tyranny:

> We are led, by events and common sense, to one conclusion: The survival of liberty in our land increasingly depends on the success of liberty in other lands. The best hope for peace in our world is the expansion of freedom in all the world.

America's vital interests and our deepest beliefs are now one. From the day of our Founding, we have proclaimed that every man and woman on this earth has rights, and dignity, and matchless value, because they bear the image of the Maker of Heaven and earth. Across the generations we have proclaimed the imperative of self-government, because no one is fit to be a master, and no one deserves to be a slave. Advancing these ideals is the mission that created our Nation. It is the honorable achievement of our fathers. Now it is the urgent requirement of our nation's security, and the calling of our time.

So it is the policy of the United States to seek and support the growth of democratic movements and institutions in every nation and culture, with the ultimate goal of ending tyranny in our world.[2]

Such soaring rhetoric is unhelpful, as I explained in an interview with Chris Matthews immediately after Bush's speech was delivered. The president's highly ideological oratory obfuscated America's national interests and instead argued that spreading democracy is not only the main goal of our foreign policy, but is the only means of our national survival. It isn't. While spreading democracy is noble as an abstract aspiration, we must accept that in some regions—especially in the Middle East, where the people are often more anti-American and sympathetic to Islamic fundamentalists than their governments are—we will be better off siding with authoritarian leaders. After all, in hindsight, it is hard to argue in favor of President Carter's decision to withdraw U.S. support of our own strategic ally—the Shah of Iran—because the shah had a poor human rights record. That was a mistake with gargantuan consequences, as the shah was overthrown and we now face a virulently hostile Iran, incomparably more oppressive and dangerous than the shah's Iran, that is one of the world's leading terrorist sponsors, and that is soon to acquire nuclear weapons.

While the Bush administration undoubtedly believed that Iraq possessed weapons of mass destruction and was a regional if not a greater threat, larger forces were also at play, as they always are, in the decision to go to war. The invasion of Iraq can be defended if it was largely meant as a strategic thrust against the global terrorist network and as a forceful example to persuade other rogue nations to cease their support for terrorism. This is the position that Henry Kissinger convincingly argued as early as January 2002 and that I took in a *Washington Times* column later that year.[3]

However, it's possible that this wasn't the case, and that the Bush Administration ordered the invasion after getting swept up in its own freedom-extolling rhetoric.

If Iraq can be transformed into a reasonably-functioning democracy—and it now seems that it can—America will gain a valuable ally in a crucial geostrategic area. But the war should also teach us how difficult it is to implant democracy in the Arab world. While I believe there's a good chance history will show that the Iraq War was a shrewd strategic move that strengthened America's position in the Middle East, we should remember that spreading democracy is a means to an end, and not an end in itself.

LIBERALISM

Like neo-conservatives, liberals also aim to use foreign policy for over-ambitious and highly-ideological goals. They look at the pursuit of national interest as an unpleasant relic of a less-civilized age. Today, they believe, enlightened statesmen can work out their differences through diplomacy and shows of good faith. The military, instead of securing U.S. interests, is to be used primarily for international humanitarian missions.

This was evident in the "humanitarian interventions" we undertook under President Clinton. Dispatching our military to Bosnia, Kosovo, Somalia, and Haiti, the Clinton Administration seemed to view our lack of national interest in these areas, perversely, as a justification in itself for intervention, for it proved our selfless motives. As the *New York Times* commented approvingly at the time on then-representative to the UN and later Secretary of State Madeleine Albright, "Whether or not an intervention meets the test of a 'vital national interest' is less important for her than whether the United States can do good in the world, using military power if necessary."[4]

The urge to "do good" is a driving force in the liberal worldview that tends to reap harmful consequences. Liberals harbor pretensions that they can remake the world by ignoring national interest and committing America to act as a good global citizen. This burdens our foreign policy with an impossibly ambitious agenda. America is a powerful country, and it already functions as the guarantor of international security and free trade. On top of that immodest role, it is impossible to expect the U.S. political, diplomatic, and military establishments to solve problems like hunger, civil unrest, or ethnic wars in every far-flung corner of the globe.

In an ideal world where the U.S. had unlimited government and military resources, perhaps we would make a good global charity service. But in the real world, every analyst and soldier we dedicate to humanitarian missions is one less human resource we have working to secure our national interests. We saw under the Clinton years that these kinds of distractions can be immensely costly—as the administration focused on trying to end civil strife in places like

Haiti and Somalia, rather than dealing with the real threat to our national interests and homeland security, Islamic terrorism.

America could never be described as an uncharitable nation. But the immense contributions we have made to world security—including but not limited to our sacrifices in two world wars and our leadership in the Cold War—were not demonstrations of our selflessness; we made these sacrifices because it was in our interest to keep Europe free and to defeat communism. Because America's interests coincide with those of the rest of the free world, our international interventions almost always benefit other democracies. This is how America helps the world—by pursuing our own interests.

Of course, there is a role for humanitarian aid, and the amount of foreign aid we dispense is by the far the most of any country. But we should not be passing out this aid merely for the sake of being charitable; and we certainly shouldn't be committing our troops and our entire foreign policy establishment to the cause of "uplifting" others. Aid should be given when it helps America. For example, our African aid policy is tied to good government practices, which is as it should be, encouraging stable and responsible governments and free trade, and in the process lessening the attraction of al Qaeda, which is looking to expand in Africa.

While liberals are enthusiastic to use the military for humanitarian missions, they are reluctant to employ armed force to secure U.S. interests, clinging instead to a blind faith in the power of diplomacy. No one personifies this tendency better than Barack Obama, whose solutions to our foreign policy challenges assume that the magnetic force of his personality will suffice to solve our biggest foreign policy challenges and to bring international miscreants to heel. In Iraq he proposes to withdraw U.S. troops in sixteen months, leaving only a small "residual force" with no military bases. Of course, one might argue, removing U.S. troops would unravel all the hard-earned progress we have made, allow the jihadists to run free, and plunge Iraq into a sectarian bloodbath. President Obama believes otherwise. He believes our withdrawal would "encourage political accommodation," "press Iraq's leaders to take responsibility for their future," and "engage" Iraqis to "forge compromises" on all the key issues of internal dispute.[5]

Perhaps he is right, but a pragmatist would say that rapidly withdrawing U.S. troops removes the biggest source of leverage we have to compel Iraqis to cooperate with one another. Expressions of good faith and Obama's personal charisma are unlikely to be as powerful.

When it comes to Iran's scheme to dominate the Persian Gulf by acquiring nuclear weapons, Obama promises to unleash "tough, direct presidential diplomacy with Iran without preconditions." Although he has in the past warned that he "will not take the military option off the table" with regard to Iran,[6] he has backed off this warning. Talk of a military option is absent from his official plan on Iran, which instead stresses the need for a "comprehensive settlement" with the mullahs.[7]

He promises to make headway on the Israeli-Palestinian conflict by making "a sustained push" to achieve peace based on a two-state solution, one state for Israel, one for the Palestinians.[8] Not a few presidents have kidded themselves that they could resolve the conflicts of the Middle East. But one worries that President Obama might be the most naïve president we've had since Jimmy Carter. There's no problem, it appears, which can't be solved by Obama's magical presence, sitting down at the table with our enemies and hashing things out. With this kind of child-like faith in the power of dialogue, it's no wonder Obama's own running mate predicted that within six months of taking office, Obama would face a foreign policy crisis manufactured solely to test his mettle.

ISOLATIONISTS AND REALISTS

The foreign policy schools of "isolationism" and "realism" have both fallen out of favor in recent years, but the difficulties of the Iraq War have given a boost to their prominent advocates, most of whom counseled against the war.

Isolationists aim to use foreign policy not to improve the world, as neo-conservatives and liberals do, but to remake America. This school of thought has not received much attention since America emerged from World War II as a superpower with global responsibilities, but it has lately been enjoying a resurgence with the quixotic presidential campaign of Ron Paul, who supports the overall redeployment of overseas troops back to America and the radical downsizing of both the military and the intelligence services. He advocates a new reliance on peaceful international trade to guarantee our prosperity, as opposed to the current policy of "meddling" in other countries' affairs. "We should let the best measure of our American greatness come from free and peaceful trade with other nations, not from displays of our military might," he advises.[9]

The isolationists' vision is a radical one. They believe it's possible to transform the United States into a gigantic Switzerland—a serene trading giant, at peace with all other countries and without the need for a robust military. While Ron Paul rightly identifies foreign trade as a crucial ingredient for American prosperity, he refuses to acknowledge that foreign trade in itself creates international interests for us that must be protected through military means. Right now access to foreign energy supplies is a crucial interest, which is the reason for much of our engagement in the Middle East. What exactly do isolationists propose we do if a nation, for whatever reason, threatens our energy supply or our trading routes? What should we do if the Islamic fundamentalist mullahs running Iran, in a quest to expand their global influence and strike a blow against the infidel West, cut off much of our oil supply by shutting down the Strait of Hormuz?

The isolationists respond that the mullahs would only do that if we, through our own policies, somehow goaded them into it. This overall premise—that a foreign government would never antagonize America without cause—can only be supported by a highly tendentious reading of American history that attributes all our foreign conflicts to American provocations. Thus, isolationism tends to degenerate into a dogmatic anti-Americanism in which our enemies, whether Nazi Germany or today's Iran—are always portrayed as innocent victims of U.S. machinations. My good friend Pat Buchanan's recent book blaming World War II mostly on our wartime ally, Great Britain, is another variation of this theme.[10]

Of all the schools of thought on foreign policy, the realists come closest to having a proper appreciation for the limitations of foreign policy and the risks of excessive ideology. Closely associated with Republican diplomatic giant Henry Kissinger, realism properly encourages American leaders to focus foreign policy on securing the national interests of the United States, with little mind paid to grander schemes of spreading our values or encouraging regimes to treat their people humanely.

Today, however, realism is too preoccupied with diplomatic maneuvering; its adherents still seem to view politics through the prism of nineteenth-century cabinet diplomacy. This has lent to the realists a certain unrealism, as they downplay or ignore human emotion and national passions in international relations. Realists mistakenly assume that all governments are rational actors, and that foreign leaders will evaluate their own national interests in a rational way; it is not at all clear, however, that Islamic fundamentalist regimes, like Iran or Saudi Arabia, are rational actors. The Saudis, for example, depend for their security on the United States military,

yet the Saudi regime is the chief proponent and bankroller of aggressive, expansionist Wahhabi Islam, which is violently opposed to the
infidel nations of the United States and Europe. And it is not at all
clear that the Iranian regime, which may well have realists among
its members, will not act on the fervently held apocalyptic desires of
its Islamist extremists to eradicate Israel, no matter what the cost.

Furthermore, in its extreme form realism slides dangerously close
to an amoral nihilism, becoming so wrapped up in geo-strategic
scheming that it gives short shrift to the fate of suffering peoples
who yearn to live in freedom. While American foreign policy cannot be defined by moral considerations alone, America is, at heart,
a moralistic nation, and we can never be true to ourselves if our foreign policy does not have a moral dimension to it.

PRAGMATIC INTERNATIONALISM IN ACTION

The foreign policy that I advocate as an American nationalist, pragmatic internationalism, accepts that we have a vital role to play in
international affairs but always puts American interests first. Here
is how such a policy would approach some of the pressing issues
America faces today.

The war on Islamic terrorism

This is our biggest foreign policy challenge and will likely remain
so for many years. It must be viewed as the existential battle of our
time, and as I argue in my previous book, *The West's Last Chance*,
Congress should demonstrate this country's commitment to victory
by officially declaring war on the Islamic jihadists who threaten us.

But even in this crucial arena, we should be careful not to suffuse
our campaign with excessive ideology. What this means, first of all,

is that it's a mistake for the president to declare war on "terrorists" everywhere, because not all terrorists threaten us or our interests. While the use of terrorism is to be condemned in all cases, the declaration of an ideological war against "terrorists" creates the expectation that we'll oppose all terrorist groups with equal energy. But in fact, there's no point in diverting our resources to counter every group everywhere that resorts to terrorism. Our war is against one specific kind of terrorist that threatens us—Islamic jihadists—and we should make this point explicit, regardless of any hurt feelings that may result from using such politically incorrect terminology.

Secondly, while democractization may be a good long-term strategy to drain the terrorist swamp, democracy takes a long time to take hold. To keep the upper-hand against Islamic terrorists in the near future, we need to make clear to them our willingness, regardless of any considerations of spreading democracy, to take additional military action throughout the globe whenever it's required. When we showed this kind of determination with the invasion of Iraq, we sent out a strong message that support for terrorism and the development of weapons of mass destruction by rogue states won't be tolerated. Libya, for one, got that message loud and clear, and decided to abandon completely its weapons of mass destruction program and undertake a new rapprochement with the West.

However, as the undermanned U.S. effort in Iraq bogged down, hostile regimes like Iran felt emboldened, ratcheting up its own nuclear program, confident that the United States was preoccupied with the war in Iraq and hobbled by growing opposition to the war in Washington, especially among Democrats like our current president. President Obama must now decide what to do about the Iranian regime. America's current strategy of Allied-led diplomacy is fine, but it will need the ultimate sanction of American force if it is to succeed—and we need to develop, if we do not yet have, the capacity to end Iran's ambitions for nuclear weapons.

As we fight Islamic jihadists, we cannot get so swept up in our rhetoric of freedom that we lose the ability to make necessary compromises and cooperate with some unsavory regimes. A good example can be found in Uzbekistan, a former Soviet republic that after September 11 became a close U.S. ally in the war on Islamic terrorism. But because of American criticism of his human rights record, Uzbek president Islom Karimov shut down the Uzbek airbase we were using for the war in Afghanistan. Our moralizing cost us a valuable ally and in the end did nothing to improve Karimov's human rights record, since he simply re-aligned Uzbekistan with Russia, which made no human rights demands at all. We must be careful not to make the same mistake in Pakistan, where the government of newly elected Pakistani president Asif Ali Zardari has shown a surprising determination to confront and defeat the Taliban on Pakistani territory. This government deserves our support even if Zardari turns out not to rule as the human rights champion he claimed to be while in the opposition.

And finally, it is crucial that we work closely with the ruling party in Turkey, the Justice and Development Party (AKP), despite its attempts to expand the role of Islam in Turkish life. While this kind of soft-Islamist program moves Turkey in the wrong direction, the AKP is a popular party that has proven its ability to govern responsibly, and I've learned from my personal meetings with top AKP officials that they are people with whom we can cooperate. Even though it would be preferable for Turkey to be governed by one of its secular parties, the truth is that during their time in power the secularists compromised themselves by corruption and economic mismanagement. Various secular institutions, from the army to the courts, periodically attempt to dislodge the AKP from power, and

America should condemn these ventures, despite their being employed against Islamism. Even under the AKP, Turkey has remained one of the few, perhaps the only, Islamic country genuinely committed to integration with the West, and these tendencies should be further encouraged.

Russia

Although Vladimir Putin has been officially downgraded from president to prime minister, it's clear that the old KGB hand still calls the shots. While it's difficult to deal with a leader as crafty and ruthless as Putin, the flipside is that his primary foreign policy goals are crystal clear: to increase Russia's influence vis-a-vis the West, and to re-establish Russia's sphere of influence over the former Soviet republics that are now, at least formally, independent nations.

Putin's Russia presents a challenge that we must handle intelligently and carefully. We should begin by acknowledging the strategic challenge that Putin poses, especially since he views much of the contest for influence in the former Soviet republics as a direct rivalry between Russia and the West—particularly America. America's policy since the fall of the Soviet Union has been to expand the West's influence as much as possible throughout the former communist bloc, especially by extending NATO membership to former communist countries. This was a sensible policy geared toward fulfilling the wishes of formerly captive East European countries to integrate fully in Western institutions—where they rightly belong—and toward increasing our own political influence, trading opportunities, and access to the crucial energy supplies of Central Asia.

Russia's opposition to this policy was easily ignored throughout most of the 1990s and 2000s, since the country was economically devastated and presided over a collapsing military that was bogged down in Chechnya for years. But under Putin all that has changed.

By deftly exploiting Russia's energy supply, Putin stabilized the economy and built up a huge surplus increasingly dedicated to strengthening the military. While the Russian army remains a shadow of the Soviet-era goliath, the government's plans to boost defense spending by an impressive 25 percent in 2009, followed by more increases over the following two years, show Putin's determination to reassert Russian power on the world stage.[11] Russia's symbolic displays of military cooperation with our biggest rival in the Western hemisphere, Venezuela, including the Kremlin's dispatch of strategic bombers and warships to our hemisphere for joint training exercises with Chavez's military, serve the same ends.

The Russian invasion of Georgia in August 2008 revealed major problems in our Russia policy. By arming and training the Georgian army and lobbying for Georgian membership in NATO, America rightly conveyed our interest in protecting Georgian independence and advancing its integration with the West. We failed, however, to back up that fine expression with any meaningful force. The Russians saw that our commitment to Georgia was mostly symbolic, moved in, and effectively annexed two regions of the country, meeting hardly any resistance from the West other than outraged speeches (along with a less-aggrieved reaction from Germany and other European countries heavily dependent on Russian energy supplies).

If we are to give real meaning to our declared interest in keeping Georgia, along with Western-leaning Ukraine, free, democratic, and within the Western sphere of influence, we need to support our statements with real force. When we pronounce our commitment to something but refuse to back it up, we look like the "weak horse" of bin Laden's rhetoric—and in Georgia, that's exactly what the Russian invasion revealed us to be.

If we're not willing to make a strategic commitment to Georgia and Ukraine, then we shouldn't pretend that we are. The Georgian fiasco sent a message to all the former Soviet republics of the Caucuses and Central Asia that the United States is afraid to use force to defend its interests while Russia is not. It is no wonder, then, that NATO's new, Eastern European members are beginning to question whether NATO even has the will to follow through on its collective security guarantee to defend any member of the alliance in case of attack.[12] With strategically important, energy-rich countries like Kazakhstan being courted by both Russia and America, which side do you think they will lean toward after seeing the contrast between Russian military might and Western weakness in Georgia?

If the United States fully acknowledges our interest in drawing the former Soviet republics away from the Russian orbit and into the Western sphere, we need to demonstrate our commitment the only way that really counts—militarily. NATO's consideration of creating a rapid-reaction force specifically to counter future aggressive moves by Russia is a good beginning that should be followed up by a more robust positioning of U.S. and NATO troops in the Central Asian and Caucasian countries that are threatened by Russian aggression.[13] This would not substantially increase the risk of a NATO war with Russia, since neither side has any interest in a direct armed conflict—especially Russia, the weaker side. Additionally, we should proceed with due speed in stationing a missile defense shield in Eastern Europe, notwithstanding Russia's blustering threats to undertake countermeasures of its own. For if we want to secure the freedom of the former Soviet republics, we need to give Russia a powerful disincentive to undertaking any more adventures.

China

China, with its huge army, incipient blue water navy, and rapidly growing economic might, represents another strategic challenge. Americans have reason to harbor a good deal of ideological hostility toward China; it's the world's largest communist country, with a brutal history of massacring its own people; it acts belligerently toward our ally Taiwan, at which it currently has pointed around 1,000 ballistic missiles; and it provides a negative, authoritarian model of modernization that is anathema to American values of freedom and democracy. What's more, with its rapid economic development in recent years, China is growing more politically assertive and no longer conceals its dream of avenging its nineteenth-century humiliations at the hands of the West. Having met with political leaders, businessmen, and ordinary people on several recent trips to China, I can honestly say that I have never met a more nationalistic and confident—I would even say cocky—people anywhere in the world.

Nevertheless, we must tread carefully with this likely future superpower. Above all else, we must recognize that at least at this point, China is much more an economic competitor to the United States than a strategic political threat. Times have changed since the Cold War, when international affairs consisted largely of zero-sum competition between the communist bloc and the free West. Although it remains a repressive one-party dictatorship, China has abandoned whatever ideological commitment it once had to overthrowing world capitalism. The regime is now mostly focused on China's economic development, which was sparked by a series of free market reforms. While it's unlikely that economic growth will result in the collapse of communism, as some free-market optimists argue, our foreign policy should not turn China into an unnecessary ideological enemy.

It is true, however, that China holds out its mold of development—authoritative capitalism—as more effective than our model of democratic capitalism, so we are in economic, cultural, and diplomatic competition with China. And in this war of ideas, we should not shy away from pointing out China's shortcomings to the developing world. We want the world to find itself in alliance with us, not with China. But again we should view ourselves as competitors, not enemies.

Adopting an overly aggressive policy toward China would be to repeat the same mistake that Britain made in the nineteenth century vis-a-vis Germany. Until the late 1800s, Britain had maintained a highly beneficial alliance with Prussia and later, a unified Germany. But Britain grew concerned when Germany began undergoing rapid industrialization and breakneck economic growth. Perceiving Germany's growing economic might as a threat, Britain began building up its military and seeking new allies such as Russia to help contain Germany, even though there was no fundamental clash in national interests between the two nations. Rightly sensing that Britain's build-up was aimed at Germany, the Kaiser began expanding Germany's military, raising tensions between the two sides. Their clashing interests were exaggerated while their common interests were downplayed, and an historic alliance gave way to the tragedies of World War I and World War II.

Historically, China has sought to dominate its own region but has evinced little enthusiasm for expanding outside the Middle Kingdom. Aside from Taiwan, if the Chinese Communists today show an interest in expanding anywhere, it is over China's northeastern border into the sparsely populated regions of southeastern Russia. Any ambitions it has in that region surely present no threat to American interests. Our relationship with China should be governed by a combination of cooperation (such as in mutually beneficial trade) and competition. But we should not take any steps that would unnecessarily provoke this looming power. We should proceed according to President Reagan's old dictum: trust, but verify.

INTERNATIONAL LAW

A key component of pragmatic internationalism is the defense of American sovereignty. Liberals, such as those who now dominate our government, are unnecessarily keen to surrender American sovereignty to international bodies and institutions. We see this mostly today with the issue of global warming, the much-hyped threat that liberals and green extremists hope to use to subject America to intrusive international treaties. It can also be seen in the way that liberals make a fetish out of the United Nations, insisting that we secure UN approval for key aspects of our foreign policy (or in John Kerry's words, that American policy should pass "the global test").

As long as international treaties or conventions serve America's interests, there can be no objection to them. For example, in an age in which nuclear proliferation threatens our national security, the Nuclear Non-Proliferation Treaty is a valuable agreement to help keep nuclear weapons out of the hands of rogue states. We cannot rely entirely on the treaty to fight proliferation, as testified by Iran's ongoing nuclear program. But even in such cases the treaty helps to marshal international support to counter these kinds of activities by rouge nations.

There is no point, however, in acquiescing to international bodies that simply arrogate to themselves new powers over sovereign countries. Many of these attempts to usurp national sovereignty come under the cloak of "human rights" or some other noble sounding endeavor, but their real goal is usually to restrain American power or to replace the legislative decisions of democratically elected national bodies with diktats from unelected international bodies or courts.

The end result is the subordination of America's interests to those of the ephemeral "international community." For example, the

Kyoto climate change treaty, had we signed it, would have placed draconian restrictions on our economic development and energy usage. And if we were to sign the current Law of the Sea Treaty, its vague requirements for anti-pollution measures could be seized upon by environmental groups to prohibit American companies from pursuing off-shore energy exploration. Other treaties and international institutions seek to subordinate our judicial system to "international norms." Chief among these is the International Criminal Court, whose mandate the United States has rightly resisted. There are also the arrogant attempts by European justices to claim "universal jurisdiction" to try anyone, anywhere in the world, on charges of genocide or other heinous crimes. This authority was most recently claimed by Spain and Belgium, although the Belgians were forced to abandon these pretenses in 2003 after scores of people began filing criminal complaints against George H. W. Bush, Colin Powell, Ariel Sharon, and other predictable targets.

Despite liberals' ritual condemnations of George W. Bush as a dangerous unilateralist, even he compromised American sovereignty when he demanded that the state of Texas rehear the case of Jose Ernesto Medellin, a Mexican national convicted of the 1993 gang rape and murder of two American girls. The Mexican government appealed Medellin's conviction to the International Court of Justice, arguing that the United States violated international treaties by failing to inform Medellin of his right to call Mexican consular officials following his arrest. After the international court ordered the "review and reconsideration" of Medellin's sentence along with those of forty-three other Mexicans on death row, Bush ordered his home state to comply with the ruling. This executive order was rejected by a Texas Appeals court and ultimately by the Supreme Court, so sanity prevailed.[14]

It's disturbing, to say the least, to see an American president support an international court's claim to authority over the American judicial system. But it should not be surprising in light of the tremendous international pressure that is now exerted on American leaders to cede U.S. sovereignty to international bodies—indeed, the European Union and multiple human rights groups supported Medellin's appeal.[15] The fact that this pressure comes from our allies as well as our international rivals makes these entreaties extremely difficult for an American president to resist.

But resist them any American president must, although it appears unlikely that President Obama will have the fortitude to do so. Obama will face enormous pressure to live up to his constant campaign vows to restore America's allegedly tattered international relationships. With his unshakeable belief in apocalyptic global warming and his emphasis on civil rights as opposed to American national security, he can hardly be expected to stand up for American sovereignty when he faces demands that the United States submit to international norms on these issues and others. After all, this is a man who opened his much-publicized speech in Berlin by pronouncing himself "a proud citizen of the United States, and a fellow citizen of the world."

Obama strongly indicates that he takes his world citizenship seriously. His rhetoric on restoring America's standing in the world emphasizes how America needs to make amends with the international community, giving scant attention, if any, to the defense of American sovereignty. For example, in a major statement of his foreign policy vision he wrote,

> To renew American leadership in the world, I intend to
> rebuild the alliances, partnerships, and institutions necessary

to confront common threats and enhance common security. Needed reform of these alliances and institutions will not come by bullying other countries to ratify changes we hatch in isolation. It will come when we convince other governments and peoples that they, too, have a stake in effective partnerships.

Too often we have sent the opposite signal to our international partners. In the case of Europe, we dismissed European reservations about the wisdom and necessity of the Iraq war. In Asia, we belittled South Korean efforts to improve relations with the North. In Latin America, from Mexico to Argentina, we failed to adequately address concerns about immigration and equity and economic growth. In Africa, we have allowed genocide to persist for over four years in Darfur and have not done nearly enough to answer the African Union's call for more support to stop the killing. I will rebuild our ties to our allies in Europe and Asia and strengthen our partnerships throughout the Americas and Africa.[16]

Few Americans would oppose the notion of strengthening our alliances and international partnerships. But this shouldn't be achieved by an apologetic president sacrificing American interests and American sovereignty to mollify a foreign constituency. If President Obama yields on these points, those of us who oppose such concessions on sovereignty must make the loudest protest of our president's actions.

American foreign policy must steadfastly resist any encroachments on U.S. sovereignty, for the erosion of our independence will inevitably further chip away at our national unity. Americans' deep, abiding loyalty to our country has traditionally been the ultimate source of America's strength. It is what binds us together and allows us to rise as one people to meet dire challenges ranging from war to economic dislocation. This national unity, though becoming increasingly brittle, is sustained by our shared history, culture, and sense of common destiny. But it's also maintained by our commitment to democratic self-rule, which will be severely weakened if the United States government begins ceding its authority piecemeal to international authorities.

In fact, this process of whittling away national identities has already begun in Europe, where the surrender of power by national governments to the European Union bureaucracy has actually reinvigorated separatist movements in Scotland, Belgium, Spain, and other countries. As Jonah Goldberg notes, the EU has made it easier for small ethnic enclaves to survive as independent states, since they can rely on the EU to carry out many of the responsibilities previously consigned to their national governments. In his words,

> By scaling back the job description of a nation-state to a few ceremonial duties, ethnic minorities see fewer risks and a lot more rewards in breaking away. Countries such as Slovakia get to trade on their votes in the EU and the U.N. They get their own anthems and sports teams and get to teach their own language and culture. It's like a McDonald's franchise. You man the register and keep the bathrooms clean, but the folks at corporate HQ do the heavy lifting. That's why the Basques, Scots and Flemings are looking to open their own franchises. The question is whether the nationalist hunger of such McNations can be satisfied by just the symbolism of autonomy.[17]

The internationalist agenda is a dangerous trend being pushed forward by elite political classes against the clearly expressed wishes of the electoral bodies of nation states. There is no better example than in Europe, where two referenda on a new EU constitution that would further empower the EU bureaucracy at the expense of national governments were rejected by the people of France and the Netherlands—two countries whose governments vociferously supported the constitution. The rejections should have been the end of the matter, since the constitution had to be ratified by all EU states before it took effect. But the EU elite would not let mere democratic procedures and popular opposition derail such an important project. So the constitution was reclassified as a "treaty"—the Treaty of Lisbon—which allowed many national governments to ratify it without submitting it to a vote of their own people. Ireland, however, insisted on holding a referendum on the treaty—it was the only country to do so—and Irish voters promptly rejected it. With imperial arrogance, French President Nicolas Sarkozy demanded that Ireland revote and approve the treaty.

There can be little doubt that by hook or by crook, the EU elites will somehow get their "treaty" approved. But in allowing a distant bureaucracy to once again run roughshod over the will of their own people, European national governments are just proving their own irrelevance. And as these governments erase themselves, Europeans will not transfer their loyalty to the distant EU bureaucracy in Brussels, but rather to a more local level—their region or ethnic group. The bloody ethnic wars that broke out with the weakening and collapse of communist regimes—in the former Yugoslavia, Azerbaijan, Georgia, and Chechnya, to name a few—show the enduring power of tribalism, especially when the authority of a national government begins to slacken.

Supranational institutions simply won't fill the emotional void that arises when a people abandons its loyalty to its own country. In countries where people of different religions or ethnicities live together, or where people retain strong regional identities, the best that can be hoped for is a peaceful separation along the lines of the former Czechoslovakia. That kind of velvet divorce, however, is more the exception than the rule.

It's best not to open the door at all to this kind of social fragmentation. America should always consult closely with its allies on important foreign policy decisions, and use diplomacy to secure the widest possible international support for American actions. But we must vehemently reject demands that would impinge on our sovereignty, even when such demands come from our own allies. The international union that liberals envision is ultimately a utopian pipedream. The best guarantor of security for the world's democracies and of free international trade is not the United Nations, but the United States military.[18]

CHAPTER 8

★ ★ ★

BROADCASTING LIBERTY

"WE ARE UNABLE TO COMMUNICATE TO THE WORLD EFFEC- tively who we are and what we stand for as a society and culture, about freedom and democracy, and about our goals and aspirations."

The foregoing was not the rash charge of some anti-Bush parti- san. Sadly, it was the considered conclusion of President Bush's Department of Defense in June 2008—seven years after we were presumably awoken from our slumber on September 11, 2001.[1]

We have taken the fight to the enemy on the battlefield, but we have neglected another crucial arena in the war on Islamic terror- ism—the battle of ideas. It is inexcusable that we have failed to do

This chapter is based on ideas put forward in a report entitled "Reforming U.S. Public Diplomacy for the 21st Century," prepared by a research team I headed at the Heritage Foundation. The team also included Helle Dale and Oliver Horn. The opinions expressed in this chapter are mine, not necessarily those of Heritage Foun- dation or my associates there.

abroad what our private sector has long led the world at: advertising, public relations, communications, creating enticing images, mass communication, broadcasting, narrow casting, shrewd use of the Internet, cell phone text messaging, direct mailing techniques, and exploitation of film, television, radio, and book publishing.

The United States government's inability to communicate our values and motivations to the world has been cruelly exploited by our enemies, who understand the vital importance of this arena. In 2005, al Qaeda deputy Ayman al-Zawahiri declared that "more than half of this battle is taking place in the battlefield of the media. We are in a media battle, a race for the hearts and minds of our Umma [the Muslim people.]"

After the invasion of Iraq, the Islamic militants gained the upper hand by spreading a simple narrative that portrayed U.S. troops as brutal oppressors and the terrorists themselves as noble resisters. Of course, in reality, the terrorists wantonly murder their fellow countrymen while U.S. troops foster democratic government. But the militants' effective communications campaign decisively influenced Iraqi public opinion. As Radio Free Europe concluded,

> Insurgent media seeks to create an alternative reality to win hearts and minds, and they are having a considerable degree of success...media outlets and products created by Sunni insurgents, who are responsible for the majority of U.S. combat deaths in Iraq, and their supporters are undermining the authority of the Iraqi government, demonizing coalition forces, fomenting sectarian strife, glorifying terrorism, and perpetuating falsehoods that obscure the accounts of responsible journalists.[2]

The terrorists' message was amplified in the mainstream Arab media and spread throughout the Muslim world. So effective were these methods that ground operations against Americans were often carried out for the sole purpose of creating a media event. The enemy's media campaign even reached America, where anti-war groups portrayed the terrorists as brave rebels ("They are the REVOLUTION, the Minutemen," declared Michael Moore) resisting dastardly U.S. troops—a view that simply confirmed their own ideological predispositions.

Of course, the indefensible abuses committed by U.S. troops at Abu Ghraib offered tremendous support to this narrative. The photos, disseminated worldwide, of naked or hooded Iraqi prisoners suffering all manner of cruelty and humiliation proved a bigger blow to the U.S. war effort than any military attack by the enemy. These images galvanized worldwide opposition to America, tainting the entire war effort in the minds of many.

Nevertheless, a government has to handle competently the outbreak of a scandal during wartime, and this the United States failed to do. The media campaign waged by Iraqi terrorists had already prepped world opinion to believe the worst about the U.S. military. The U.S. government did not effectively communicate the message that such abuses, perpetrated by roughly a dozen soldiers, were in no way representative of the behavior of the U.S. military, and that the perpetrators were investigated and punished accordingly. Lacking an effective communications campaign, the government allowed an abuse scandal at one prison to overshadow the far bloodier outrages of Iraqi terrorists, such as the wholesale massacre of innocents in numerous mosque bombings.

The government would induce less opposition both at home and abroad if it were able to show to the world the true nature of our good conduct (so long as our conduct is actually good). Good faith objections to U.S. government action are spawned by our incompetence at accurately portraying our war effort to Iraqis, the international community, and our own public. While some people—both at home and abroad—will oppose any and all U.S. military action, a critical mass will form their opinions based on the specific information they receive. We can no longer afford to cede to our enemies the communications war over this large swathe of people.

After an arduous struggle, thanks to the surge it now appears that victory in Iraq is within our grasp. But one should note that a key element of the surge was that it enhanced our direct communication with the Iraqi people as we sent larger numbers of troops into cities, towns, and villages. As the Iraqis saw firsthand our troops providing security against the death squads that were terrorizing the population and also benevolently dispensing humanitarian aid, Iraqi support for the Americans grew, and the Iraqi population become more determined to defeat the terrorists

While those who conduct our future wars and occupations will, I hope, learn from the successful tactics implemented in Iraq by General Petraeus, they must not ignore the crucial communications aspect, for mass communication has become a key element not only of modern warfare, but of international diplomacy overall. It has become a matter of national urgency that we adopt an effective strategic communications campaign not only as an integral part of our war efforts, but also to demonstrate to the world our fundamental decency and our role as an advocate on behalf of free people.

LESSONS FROM HISTORY

It's hard to believe that the U.S. government today does not understand the value of mass communication. This is a lesson learned long ago by history's dominating figures. Even the most extreme egomaniacs and the most ruthless military conquerors—Alexander the Great, Attila the Hun, Genghis Khan, Napoleon, Lenin, Stalin, and Hitler—understood that it's not only easier to win by persuasion than by the sword, but it's a more certain conquest.

But decent, democratic nations tend simply to assume that the world will see their virtues, and so they usually don't even bother to make their case in a systematic way. We Americans usually ignore the broader world, only engaging in sustained communications when danger lurks. When those moments arrive, however, we have historically been pretty effective.

Our first effort at an international communications campaign came during our revolution, when we sent Benjamin Franklin to France to drum up support for the cause of liberty. In those days, one man—admittedly one of the most compelling, charming, brilliant personalities to arise in our land—was able to win not only France's admiration, but her navy, troops and material as well.

Since then, America has typically ramped up communications efforts during wartime and abolished them once the danger has passed. Some of these campaigns were better than others. During World War I, President Woodrow Wilson's "Creel" Committee, officially named the Committee on Public Information, was created in a misguided communications campaign aimed solely at the domestic population. Notoriously, one of Wilson's top advisors, Edward Bernays, described the committee's mission as "engineering consent" for the war effort. With that as its stated goal, it's unsurprising that the committee turned into a lying propaganda mill aimed at U.S. citizens. During World War II a much more effective information agency was created—the Office of War Information. Geared at both domestic and foreign opinion, the office contrasted American liberty with fascist oppression sharply and unapologetically in billboards, placards, news shorts, radio series, and the like.

The Cold War brought about a much more sustained international information campaign directed by the United States Information Agency (USIA). Created in 1953 by President Eisenhower, the USIA for four decades led our communications efforts as we engaged in a life-or-death struggle against Soviet communism for the hearts and minds of the world's people. The Soviets had their own enormous propaganda campaign aimed against America's "heartless capitalism," dedicating vast resources to the effort and reaching out to foreign countries through a number of major agencies and organizations, most notably the Cominform (successor to the pre–World War II Comintern).

In light of the Soviet Union's eventual economic and political collapse, it's hard to believe that during the Cold War, tens of millions of people throughout the world really believed Soviet propaganda that proclaimed the economic superiority of communism over the free market. The all-encompassing poverty and political oppression that always characterized the Soviet Union should have made it obvious to any level-headed observer that communism was a grossly inefficient and inherently oppressive system. And yet, the communists' propaganda convinced people ranging from third-world peasants to American plutocrats that history was on their side. Soviet leader Nikita Khrushchev became famous for his 1959 exclamation that the Soviets would out-produce us, "bury" us, and that our children would live under communism. What's less well-remembered is that at the time, many people actually believed him.

The USIA faced a monumental challenge in countering the Soviet propaganda machine, but the U.S. government fully recognized the importance of the ideological competition. Rising to the occasion, the USIA indefatigably championed the ideals of democracy, individual rights, and free markets. According to Dr. Carnes Lord, who crafted President Reagan's public diplomacy strategy, the "promotion of these values contributed mightily to the nearly bloodless dissolution of the Soviet Empire."[3] This sentiment is affirmed by the Eastern European dissidents who led the battle against communism; renowned dissident and former Czech president Vaclav Havel credited Radio Free Europe, which broadcast American values direct to the captive peoples of the communist bloc, with galvanizing opposition to communist rule.[4]

After the fall of the Soviet Union many Americans, both within and outside of the government, believed that we had arrived at the "end of history." With America seeming to have won decisively the battle of ideas, people were anxious to reap the expected "peace dividend." In addition to slashing the size of our army by 40 percent, we phased out most of our communications effort. Most critically, in 1999 President Clinton and Congress dismantled the USIA and dispersed its thousands of employees and their budgets throughout the government.

This move upheld a tradition of similar decisions through American history. After World War I, not only was the Creel Committee rightfully shut down, but we sunk part of our own naval fleet in the delusional belief that we had just won "the war to end all wars." Likewise, after World War II, the Office of War Information was abolished. In each of these instances, Americans acted on the belief that the need to influence world opinion ended when the guns went silent.

The Iraq War revealed that belief to be mistaken. Thrust suddenly into war, we lacked a comprehensive mechanism for effectively making the case for our values and motivations. The Cold War communications apparatus had mostly been disbanded, with nothing left over readily to take its place. As a result, we ceded the communications battle to our enemies and suffered the attendant consequences.

WHAT WE HAVE HERE IS A FAILURE TO COMMUNICATE

I first realized how far our communications capacities have degraded shortly after the September 11 attacks. Having worked as a speechwriter, polling analyst, and communications strategist on President Ronald Reagan's White House staff, and later having led Speaker Newt Gingrich and the congressional Republicans' national communications team in the 1990s, I naturally paid close attention to how our government communicated after we suffered the biggest terrorist attack on the American homeland in history.

Following the initial shock, I expected to see a reasonably systematic message coming from the government regarding the nature of the threat, the steps we were taking to address it, and the national and cultural values involved in our new struggle. I realized, however, that in an enterprise as large as the United States government there can never be a seamless message or perfect coordination among its many parts. Having taken part in such efforts, I am particularly sympathetic to the difficulty of making the whole thing hang together.

But as the months passed, I noticed that rather than tending to come together, the system seemed to become more incoherent. On any given day the messages coming out of the Pentagon, the State Department, the Treasury, and the White House seemed discordant—sometimes explicitly at odds with each other. I started keeping track of what our senior ambassadors were saying abroad, and saw no evidence of any effort to coordinate messages.

I called up some old friends in the government—senior career people involved in national security, intelligence, defense, anti-terrorism, and communications matters. I asked if they were coordinating efforts as we had in the Reagan White House, when national security communications were directed out of a special unit of the president's Nationals Security Council staff. I was told there was no functioning interagency communications operation at all.

This is a vital undertaking that we neglect at our own peril. We are now in a long struggle to protect our people and our country from the very real threat of terrorist attack, possibly involving weapons of mass destruction. Such a terrible attack is made more likely by the broad support the attackers have amongst their people. While only the smallest fraction of the world's 1.4 billion Muslims would be prone to such violence, the harshly negative view most Muslims have of America creates a safer haven for the terrorists than should be the case—and makes the world more dangerous for us.

For example, the results of a major study issued in April 2007 by a respected team at the University of Maryland's World Public Opinion show that the Muslim world is grossly misinformed about American motivations and intentions in key foreign policy issues. Consider the following polling results:

- *Do you think a goal of US foreign policy is to weaken and divide the Islamic world?*

Moroccans	Yes	78%	No	11%
Egyptians	Yes	92%	No	4%
Pakistanis	Yes	73%	No	9%
Indonesians	Yes	73%	No	15%

- *Do you think a goal of U.S. foreign policy is to spread Christianity to the Middle East?*

Moroccans	Yes	67%	No	22%
Pakistanis	Yes	64%	No	14%
Indonesians	Yes	61%	No	21%

- *Do you think a goal of U.S. foreign policy is to see the creation of an independent and economically viable Palestinian State?*

Moroccans	Yes	27%	No	64%
Egyptians	Yes	7%	No	97%
Pakistanis	Yes	29%	No	36%
Indonesians	Yes	30%	No	40%[5]

It is noteworthy that in all instances, the beliefs of the Muslim public are mistaken in a way likely to make people more hostile to the United States and more friendly to our enemies. But also note that the numbers vary. Muslim opinion is not monolithic—Islamic nations, like all other ones, are exposed to different kinds of information and respond in various ways based on their pre-existing base of knowledge and cultural outlook.

Remarkably, I can find no evidence that the U.S. government has ever made a systematic, comprehensive effort to communicate our intentions to the Muslim people of the Middle East on any topic— and certainly not on these three key questions. If Muslims truly believe that we're out to weaken and divide them, convert them to Christianity, and block the creation of a Palestinian state, then it begins to make sense why some of them encourage their sons to fight in the jihad against us.

We need a program to broadcast a clear, consistent message to the Muslim world: No, the U.S. government is not trying to convert

Muslims to Christianity; no, the U.S. is not trying to divide and weaken Muslims; and yes, for two decades every American administration has followed a bipartisan policy favoring the creation of an independent and economically viable Palestinian state. Until those points are widely understood, we have little reason to hope to encounter a more sympathetic audience in the Middle East.

A PLAN FOR ACTION

Aside from communicating our views and values regarding these major issues of foreign policy, we need to develop continual practices that communicate America's messages to the world effectively on a daily basis. Whenever a U.S. Secretary of State or Treasury official attends an important conference, that official should travel as part of a carefully designed and implemented communications program focused on shaping the public perception of this man and his surroundings.

Consider how effective presidential candidates or CEOs of major American corporation move through public life. Even when simply going from one place to another, they usually look poised, deliberate, and in control. This may come naturally to some, but most are coached by political and corporate communications consultants who help them to present themselves effectively to the public.

Of course, officials can take or reject a consultant's advice. But at least they should care how they are being perceived. This is simply not the case even with the top officials of our federal government. Secretaries of State routinely visit the Middle East with no more communications support than a one page press release announcing the countries they will visit and the people they will meet. As a result, perceptions of their trips are shaped by others—the mass media who cover the expeditions, and our enemies who regularly lie about our leaders' motivations and plans.

A proper plan would prepare the ground for a month or two beforehand through one-on-one briefings for senior journalists, the aggressive use of Internet communities, the solicitation of favorable public statements from friendly foreign sources, and perhaps even some assistance from our clandestine communications and psychological operatives. Trips would be coordinated among numerous government agencies to maximize any positive news that jointly affects them. And after trips end, we would work the reaction and monitor the follow up for another month or two.

U.S. government representatives participate in countless events every day that would benefit from optimally presenting them to different publics around the world. Just as every planned military event—even something as trivial as the docking of a navy ship in an allied harbor—is merely the visible tip of a comprehensive doctrine of action, so each U.S. government activity around the world should be part of a routine communications process supported by a well-trained, well-funded bureaucracy and guided by political objectives established by a chain of command that reaches the president.

Every president, vice president, senator, and congressman gained his office in large part because he had a successfully conceived and implemented strategic communications plan. So it is unsettling that once in office, politicians lose interest in applying their own successful strategies to the national security interests of our country.

Margaret Thatcher once said that America is the only nation in the world "built upon an idea." This idea—liberty—has transcended geography and ethnicity to shape American identity and to inspire political discourse, both domestic and foreign, since the nation's founding nearly two and a half centuries ago. Indeed, it was

John Adams who wrote that the American Revolution occurred first "in the hearts and minds of the people." Ideas lie at the very core of this country. It is both frustrating and ironic, therefore, that the United States should fail so miserably at conveying ideas today.[6]

CHAPTER 9

★   ★   ★

BACK TO BASICS: READING, WRITING, AND ROTC

A NATION'S DESTINY LIES IN ITS EDUCATION SYSTEM—THAT AXIOM has been recognized at least since the time of the ancient Greeks. As Aristotle observed, "All who have meditated on the art of governing mankind have been convinced that the fate of empires depends on the education of the youth." This adage should be at the forefront of the thinking of every American nationalist. Although our attention is necessarily focused on the many foreign threats that now confront our nation, we can no longer ignore the critical challenge we face here at home in educating our children to cherish their American heritage. For even the most effective foreign policy, the most secure energy supply, and the fiercest army cannot save a democratic republic once the population has lost faith in its guiding principles and disowned its history.

If America is to survive and prosper, we have to teach patriotism to our future generations. For too long, schools have inculcated in our youth a politicized suspicion of our nation and a warped view of its history that dwells on America's faults and transgressions while overlooking or denigrating its accomplishments. It is an affront to our people that this outlook, having gained prominence among the academic establishment in the 1960s and '70s, has become the dominant interpretation of U.S. history propagated in our school textbooks and classrooms.

The very idea of teaching patriotism is anathema today among the academics and educators who control our nation's history curriculum. Enthralled by multiculturalism, "whole child" teaching, and other destructive dogmas, they view patriotism as a freakish, backward relic of the unenlightened, pre-1960s era. In their eyes, teaching that America is an exceptional nation worthy of exceptional pride would be to commit the cardinal sin of judgementalism.

Ensuring our children once again learn the true, remarkable history of our country should be a national priority of the highest order. We can hardly expect that future generations will be willing put their country first—or to even take an interest in how it is run—if they're taught to believe that our history is marked by little other than colonialism, racism, and class oppression. Indeed, the America that emerges from history textbooks today is largely unrecognizable to a patriot or an honest historian. The country that I love—one that has paid an enormous price to preserve and spread liberty in the world—has been replaced by a grotesque oligarchy characterized by the brutality of its government policies and the suffering of its own people.

America is not perfect, of course, and we must study our past mistakes and learn from them. But is it really justifiable that one of the most commonly recurring images used in textbooks to depict twentieth-century American life is a picture of the Ku Klux Klan?[1] A 2004 textbook survey by the American Textbook Council describes how one widely-used history textbook, Houghton Mifflin's *To See a World*, portrays America not as the sweet land of liberty where millions of immigrants have found freedom and become proud Americans, but as a heartbreaking, blighted country populated by isolated identity groups struggling to overcome oppression:

> The United States is reinvented as a "land of diversity" and "a nation of many peoples." What remains solely of America's civic being is the immigrant experience, and in keeping with its view of the American past, the book stresses hardships late nineteenth- and early twentieth century migrants faced in a hard-hearted land. In *To See a World*'s round-up chapter on North America, entitled "For the Good of All," the American vision is vested in the African-American "freedom struggles" that "helped open the door for all minorities and women." It includes a special section on identifying gender stereotypes—ridiculous or evil, you decide—and education's value, presumably, in breaking these stereotypes.[2]

In order fully to convey the injustice that allegedly pervades America, textbooks downplay the evil nature of totalitarian regimes whose encroachments we have resisted. This is particularly the case with the discussion of communism, where a frank account of the murderous results of communist rule might inadvertently justify American foreign policy during the Cold War. So textbooks list a few unsavory elements of communist despotisms while also extolling their supposed accomplishments and the generous ways that communist tyrants cared for their people (at least those they didn't kill):

> In *Connections to Today*, Soviet achievements in economic growth, increased military power, education and filmmaking

are featured. Students read little of forced labor camps or the fate of the kulaks. But at least these horrors are mentioned. For example, in a feeble passage on the Cold War, the middle-school world cultures textbook, *To See a World*, says, under the heading of "Life Behind the Iron Curtain," only the following:

"The Iron Curtain cut off contact between the people of Eastern and Western Europe. Barbed wire lined the borders. Communist governments in Eastern Europe granted their people few freedoms. Workers were told where to work. Newspapers were told what to print, teachers what to teach. In some ways these Communist governments did take care of their citizens. Food prices were low. Health care was free. Ethnic conflicts, especially in the Balkans and the Soviet Union, were reduced."[3]

While largely overlooking the tens of millions of victims starved and murdered by communists, textbooks dedicate page upon page to the alleged victims of McCarthyism, most of whom at most lost their jobs and were often, in fact, communists.

The teaching of this distorted view of history is nothing new, unfortunately—Lynne Cheney, former chairwoman of the National Endowment of the Humanities, blew the whistle on it as far back as 1994 in a *Wall Street Journal* column. In "The End of History," Cheney revealed how a draft document for new national standards for teaching history had become infected with multicultural dogmatism and anti-American bias. In the proposed standards, Joseph McCarthy and McCarthyism received nineteen references and the Ku Klux Klan got seventeen, compared to zero references to Alexander Graham Bell, Thomas Edison, Albert Einstein, and the Wright

Brothers. The standards found the establishment of the Sierra Club and the National Organization of Women worthy of mention, but not the convocation of the first U.S. Congress.[4]

Despite Cheney's best efforts, the assault on our history has spread to schools throughout the country. Inexplicably, even Republican administrations—including an administration in which Cheney's husband served as vice president—have shown little inclination to challenge the teaching of revisionist history. As a result, patriotic views have largely been eliminated from our teaching materials. America's contribution to the advance of worldwide freedom may still exist in our individual memories, but history is now being written—and taught—from a much different perspective.

THE LARGER AGENDA

What can explain this impetus, over the last decade and a half, to denigrate America to our own children? Partly, it's a result of the publishing process. Interest groups have become adept at pressuring publishers into advancing their viewpoint on various historical events and themes. Hoping to forestall any annoying criticism, publishers now routinely allow ethnic lobbies and other organizations to vet their textbooks before publication. Furthermore, the publishers themselves have developed "bias guidelines" to ensure that no minorities or other interest groups—aside, perhaps, from patriotic Americans—will be offended by the material. The result, according to the 2008 study *The Trouble with Textbooks*, is a system of self-censorship and cultural equivalence that "celebrates everybody and omits many unpleasant historical facts."[5]

One grievance group that has become influential in textbook publishing is the organized Muslim lobby. In fact, the founder of the Council on Islamic Education, the chief Islamic group for vetting

American textbooks, refers to his work as a "bloodless revolution . . . inside American junior high and high school classrooms."[6]
And indeed, it is. While one may expect textbooks to show defer-
ence to Muslims because of the demands of political correctness,
they actually go so far as to outright proselytize Islam.

As *The Trouble with Textbooks* demonstrates, textbooks relate
Christian and Jewish religious traditions as stories attributed to
some source (for example, "According to the New Testament. . ."),
while Islamic traditions are related as indisputable historical facts.
In Holt's *World History*, we read that Moses "claimed" to receive
the Ten Commandments from God, but that Mohammed simply
"received" the Koran from God. In Pearson's *World Civilizations*,
we learn that Jesus of Nazareth is "believed by Christians to be the
Messiah," but that Muhammad "received revelations from Allah."
Or consider McDougal Littell's *World Cultures and Geography*,
which relates that "Judaism is a *story* of exile" and that "Christians
believe that Jesus was the promised Messiah," but that the Koran
"*is* the collection of God's revelations to Muhammad" (emphasis
added).[7] Perhaps one such instance could be overlooked, but the
fact that the traditions of Islam—and only Islam—are repeatedly
relayed as historical truth in numerous popular textbooks indicates
that publishers have simply caved in to the demands of Islamic pressure groups. And in doing so, they have egregiously denigrated
America's Judeo-Christian heritage.

The problem would not be so entrenched if it only stemmed from
servile publishers. But something more insidious is at work. Anti-
Western and anti-American teachings form the core of the debased
theory of critical pedagogy, which aims to inculcate in our youth the
ideals of "social justice." Denying that classroom teaching can or
should be non-political, advocates of critical pedagogy openly seek
to indoctrinate students in a Marxist-inspired ideology that holds

America to be a land of rank injustice with a history dominated by racism, exploitation, and perhaps most absurdly, colonialism. They seek to use their positions in our education system to turn students into political activists dedicated to fighting the ubiquitous oppression that allegedly typifies America today.

The outwardly subversive goals of critical pedagogy make the field a welcome home for anti-American malcontents like the unrepentant domestic terrorist Bill Ayers, who presided over a string of bombings in the late 1960s and early 1970s committed by the self-styled communist guerilla group, the Weatherman Underground. Having failed in his goal of violently overthrowing the U.S. government and the entire capitalist system, Ayers completed a doctoral program in education and embraced critical pedagogy as a perfectly legal way to pursue his revolutionary goals. Now a tenured education professor at the University of Illinois at Chicago, he has become an influential advocate of social justice in the classroom. Aside from teaching classes, lecturing at various education schools, conducting teacher training and professional development for Chicago public schools, and editing a series of books, he has written several tomes on teaching social justice, including one that is a bestseller in education schools.[8]

Ayers' popularity among educators was demonstrated during the 2008 presidential campaign, when over 4,000 educators signed an on-line petition condemning the public "attacks" on the former terrorist after the news emerged that he had helped launch Barack Obama's political career.[9] (Although during his campaign Obama famously described Ayers as just "a guy who lives in my neighborhood," after the election Ayers released a revised memoir in which he admits that he and Obama were "family friends.")[10] A much more consequential—and disturbing—show of support came in March 2008, when Ayers was elected vice president for curriculum of the American Educational Research Association, America's biggest organization of education researchers. The association affirms its commitment to critical pedagogy with a "social justice mission statement" pledging to "promote social justice principles and policies in the conduct of education research."[11]

Other trendy teaching theories are also undermining our school curriculum. The most damaging of these is "whole child" teaching, in which enormous emphasis is placed on improving students' self-esteem and validating their opinions, no matter how deluded or ill-informed they may be. Thanks to this pedagogy, the rigorous teaching of facts and analytical tools is being subordinated to the goal of ensuring the tranquility of infantilized students. And far from being a fringe trend, self-esteem education has become the principal educational theory in our schools today.[12]

This therapeutic pseudo-teaching inevitably leads to a debasing of academic standards, rampant grade inflation, and the social promotion of unprepared students to the next grade (seeing as bad grades could harm a student's fragile sense of self-worth). As Thomas Sowell noted, "While school children in Japan are learning science, mathematics, and a foreign language, American school children are sitting around in circles, unburdening their psyches and 'expressing themselves' on scientific, economic and military issues for which they lack even the rudiments of competence. Worse than what they are *not* learning is what they *are* learning—presumptuous superficiality taught by the practitioners of it."[13]

Whole child teaching short-changes American students in all subjects, including history. Less than a year after the September 11 attacks, columnist George Will took a look at the guidelines developed by the National Education Association, the nation's largest teachers' union, for teaching about the massacre on its one-year anniversary. The results were a tragedy of a farce. The NEA suggested creating a "circle of feelings" as a "healing tool" to "give students the opportunity to discuss and have validated their feelings about the events of Sept. 11 in a nonjudgmental discussion circle." In case students were still feeling unvalidated after their discussion circle, they were to be instructed that "they can help themselves feel better by taking care of themselves, by following their established routines and by identifying activities that make them feel better."[14]

American teachers need to stop treating our kids like petrified, emotionally maladjusted weaklings in need of protection from the realities of history. In fact, teachers should be taking the opposite approach, working to toughen up young students in order to prepare them to meet and surmount the challenges they will face in their lifetimes. Confessing their feelings to a discussion circle may earn kids a good grade from an NEA teacher, but it's a terrible way to prepare them to become responsible, industrious adults. From the earliest possible age, kids should be taught self-reliance and how to overcome problems by thinking and acting. They should confront and begin to analyze world events, not be sheltered from them in a protective cocoon of emotional validation. They need to learn that people have responsibilities they must live up to, regardless of how it makes them feel. If we teach our youth that the entire world revolves around their emotional well-being, how can we possibly expect them to grow into good citizens capable of sacrifice, when necessary, for the good of their country?

Perhaps even more important than abolishing self-esteem pedagogy is the need to root out the insidious, anti-American doctrines of multiculturalism and critical pedagogy that pervade our schools. The hand-wringing self-indictments that permeate our history lessons should be replaced by an unashamed patriotism that relates the exceptional nature of our country, founded on the idea of liberty. The telling of American history as isolated stories of separate, struggling ethnic groups should be replaced with a narrative focused on Americans as a united people. Instead of being ignored at best or denigrated at worst, American inventors and industrialists should be lauded for their accomplishments. At every level of schooling, children should be taught to take pride in their country, faults and all, and in its Western, Judeo-Christian heritage.[15]

It would be easy enough for the government to devise new national standards for a patriotic history pedagogy and for state legislators to commission textbooks that follow those standards, but there is little political will to do so. This should not be a partisan issue; judging by the outraged reaction of liberals whenever they perceive someone to be questioning their patriotism, they should stand foursquare behind a bipartisan effort to teach it.

President Obama, however, doesn't appear to see the value in such a push. His lengthy education plan is filled with expensive new programs, but doesn't once mention the development of a patriotic curriculum.[16] Since Obama served as board chairman from 1995 to 1999 of the Chicago Annenberg Challenge, a foundation founded by Bill Ayers and dedicated to spreading social justice pedagogy, it's doubtful that we'll see Obama energetically fight against the poisonous teaching theories he once energetically promoted.[17]

JROTC: IN THE SERVICE OF PATRIOTISM

President Obama has drafted a plan to encourage American middle school and high school students to perform fifty hours of community service per year, but he's vague on what this would actually entail. His plan only recommends two specific programs for that age cohort: the YouthBuild Program, in which low-income youths repair and build low-income housing, and the "green job corps," a program he intends to create for youths to "improve energy conservation and efficiency of homes and buildings in their communities."[18] Obama is certainly correct that we should encourage the younger generation to serve their country. While building homes for the poor is a worthwhile endeavor, however, one suspects that a great deal of Obama's youth service program, like so much of his agenda, will focus on cultivating environmental awareness above any other value.

As is the case with his education plan, the word "patriotism" is absent from Obama's entire national service plan. He has no ambition to promote patriotism, even though we already have an ideal service program to achieve this goal: Junior ROTC. Once geared toward developing military recruits, JROTC now focuses on teaching good citizenship, moral development, self-discipline, physical fitness, respect for our armed forces, and personal responsibility —all key qualities that are woefully deficient in today's dominant pedagogies. Furthermore, the program offers a much more rigorous and time-tested method for reaching at-risk youths than does Obama's dubious plan to put them to work increasing "energy conservation" in other people's homes.

JROTC has grown considerably in recent years, but all the service branches combined still have less than 3,500 units. There are a number of obstacles that hinder JROTC's expansion. Since school districts split the costs of JROTC programs with the Department of Defense, some districts plausibly argue that they simply can't afford to offer JROTC. This problem can easily be rectified by the federal government covering all JROTC costs for financially-strapped school districts.

Additionally, JROTC expansion has been slowed by anti-military, pro-gay, and leftwing groups, frequently with allies serving in school district bureaucracies, who are ideologically opposed to the military. In Los Angeles, teachers joined groups like "United Students" and the "Coalition Against Militarism in Our Schools" to agitate against JROTC and military recruiters. Although it's questionable whether the personal opinions of these "educators" belong in the classroom at all, these activists are not subtle about getting them across to students. As the *Los Angeles Times* reported about one United Students teacher in Los Angeles' Roosevelt High School, "Lopez, the social studies teacher, keeps a stack of glossy brochures propped on his chalkboard titled 'Don't Die in a Dead-End Job! Information for Young People Considering the Military' that show a soldier saluting flag-draped coffins. Prominent on his wall is a poster called "Ten Points to Consider Before You Sign a Military Enlistment Agreement."[19]

This kind of outright indoctrination is proving effective—enrollment in Roosevelt's JROTC program fell 43 percent in the four years after the Coalition Against Militarism was founded. As one eleventh-grader reported, JROTC uniforms used to be admired in school. But now, "Everyone says JROTC is bad."[20]

Some JROTC opponents explain their stance as a protest against the military's "don't ask, don't tell" policy on homosexual soldiers. This was the rationale offered by members of the San Francisco Board of Education when they voted in 2006 to ban JROTC from the city's high schools. (The ban was suspended until they could develop alternative programming.) While they enjoy outsized influence in many school districts, however, anti-JROTC activists represent an extremist fringe with little public support. In 2008, San Francisco voters approved by 53 percent a measure calling for the city to keep its JROTC programs. The initiative was non-binding, meaning the board of education radicals may implement their ban anyway, but its approval in what is arguably the most anti-military city in America is evidence of broad public support for JROTC. Americans of nearly all political stripes back the program, whose opponents consistently display a festering animus toward the men and women who put their lives on the line to ensure the freedom and security of this country.

In a 2008 forum at Columbia University, Barack Obama spoke out against the host university's ban on ROTC, a popular prohibition throughout the Ivy League and other top colleges. He should take a similar stand against the unconscionable campaign against JROTC, and back up his words with a comprehensive program to expand JROTC throughout the nation.

A NEW DEAL FOR TENURED RADICALS

The pervasive ban on ROTC only scratches the surface of the deep problems plaguing our higher education system. Having seized control of the commanding heights of education, refugees from the 1960s New Left have converted our universities into a re-education gulag designed to churn out militants devoted to attacking the American way of life.

The professoriate is overwhelmingly and indisputably leftwing. A 2005 study by political scientists from the University of Toronto found that 72 percent of professors identify themselves as liberal, compared to just 15 percent who are conservatives. There is even less balance at the most elite schools, where liberal professors dominate their conservative colleagues by 87 percent to 13 percent. As the *Washington Post* noted, the study's findings indicate that "college faculties, long assumed to be a liberal bastion, lean further to the left than even the most conspiratorial conservatives might have imagined."[21]

Although professors may call themselves liberals, they actually tend toward the far left; the University of Toronto study found that 65 percent of professors believe the government should ensure full employment, a position that would be hard to distinguish from socialism. As a result of academia's ideological radicalism, politically correct pedagogies that at first seemed like bizarre anomalies have become institutionalized across our university system. "Critical race theory" and "critical legal studies" analyze American society and its legal system entirely through the prism of racial injustice; much of the humanities has been Balkanized into such ethnic ghettos as "African-American studies," "Latino studies," "women's studies," and "queer studies"; historical revisionists and practitioners of "peace studies" have reinterpreted the Cold War to cast the Soviet Union as a victim of American imperialism; and the great canon of Western literature, now viewed as the oppressive hegemony of dead white males, is being replaced in college syllabi with a multicultural slate of unknown, undistinguished writers whose sole accomplishment is that they are untainted by whiteness.

College educators have abdicated their responsibility to produce young citizens well-educated in civics. Since so many academics view America as an oppressive society based on white supremacy, they have little motivation to inculcate any sense of obligation to the country other than to change it. In a world where democrats and dissidents suffering under authoritarian regimes look to America for inspiration in the principles of liberty, our universities teach our own young men and women that we have nothing to offer the world other than a thinly veiled form of apartheid.

It should come as no surprise, then, that frequent college lecturers comprise not only far-left radicals, but also accused political criminals and convicted terrorists. In recent years, regulars on the paid college lecture circuit have included Laura Whitehorn, who served fourteen years in jail after carrying out a series of bombings in America, including an attack on the Capitol building; Elaine Brown, a former Black Panther who led the organization at a time when it was deeply involved in murder, extortion, and other serious crimes;[22] Angela Davis, a former Communist Party member who appeared on the FBI's 10 most wanted list after a fellow "revolutionary" murdered a sitting judge with a gun registered in her name. (Davis beat the charges of murder, conspiracy, and kidnapping, and for a time took up residence in Castro's Cuba); Sami al-Arian, before he pled guilty to conspiracy to aid the Palestinian Islamic Jihad terror group; and of course, the bomber Bill Ayers.

Indoctrination into academia's anti-American orthodoxy often begins as soon as freshmen arrive at a university for orientation. A typical example was catalogued by the American Council of Trustees and Alumni, which reported that in 2006 Baruch College assigned all freshmen to read a book, *War Is a Force that Gives Us Meaning*, that argues that America is "addicted to war." Afterward, students were forced to regurgitate anti-American propaganda, being made to describe what "distortions in our democracy have already taken place" since the September 11 attacks, and list ways that America has "moved away from [the virtues of humility and compassion] in the past decade."[23]

The Foundation for Individual Rights in Education (FIRE), a group that advocates for free speech on college campuses, revealed an even more intrusive exercise in thought control in 2007 at the University of Delaware, which required students staying in residence halls to undergo "treatments" that would help them to "recognize that systemic oppression exists in our society," and to understand "the benefits of dismantling systems of oppression." The program defined some of its key terms:

- Racist: "A racist is one who is both privileged and socialized on the basis of race by a white supremacist (racist) system. The term applies to all white people (i.e., people

of European descent) living in the United States, regardless of class, gender, religion, culture or sexuality."

- Reverse racism: "A term created and used by white people to deny their white privilege."
- Non-racist: "A non-term. The term was created by whites
to deny responsibility for systemic racism, to maintain an
aura of innocence in the face of racial oppression, and to
shift responsibility for that oppression from whites to
people of color."[24]

Although university radicals justify the most outrageous insults to
America and its citizens as a noble form of "dissent," they are loath
to tolerate challenges to their own political orthodoxy (which may,
in part, explain their opposition to ROTC's presence on campus).
Students who rebel against their ideological stranglehold face innu-
merable hurdles. Aside from the targets of their rebellion having
control over their grades, many campuses have erected institutional
barriers that effectively shut down their students' free speech. The
most common such barrier is speech codes, usually put forward as
"anti-discrimination" or "anti-harassment" regulations. Purporting
to protect women and minorities by outlawing offensive expressions, speech codes long ago reached the point of oppressive absur-
dity, exemplified by the infamous water buffalo incident in 1993,
when the University of Pennsylvania prosecuted a student for racial
harassment after he called a loud group of sorority sisters "water
buffalo."[25]

A single example conveys the Orwellian nature of campus speech
codes. In November 2008, FIRE announced its "speech code of the
month" belonged to the University of the Pacific, which "prohibits
any conduct 'that undermines the emotional, physical, or ethical
integrity of any community member.' This includes any expression,

'intentional or unintentional,' that 'has the effect of demeaning, ridiculing, defaming, stigmatizing, intimidating, slandering or impeding the work or movement of a person or persons or conduct that supports or parodies the oppression of others.' Examples of explicitly prohibited expression include 'insults,' 'jokes,' 'teasing,' and 'derogatory comments.'"[26]

While such regulations may seem more ridiculous than threatening, they have an explicitly political dimension. As FIRE observes, a ban on expression that parodies the oppression of others "could easily be read to include political expression such as opposition to affirmative action, illegal immigration, or gay marriage." And universities do enforce these rules against students who don't follow the party line; FIRE documents numerous universities suppressing student-sponsored bake sales staged as a satirical protest against affirmative action policies.[27]

Universities should be a tremendous asset to our national security, producing quality scholarship that helps policymakers understand the world and especially the Middle East. But academia's unremitting ideological bias has substantially reduced the value of its output—a year after the September 11 attacks, when the media, government, and general public were devouring information on Islamic terrorism, the titles of the 558 papers presented at the annual conference of the Middle Eastern Studies Association included just two references to terrorism—both of which referred to the American "war on terror," and not the actual phenomenon of terrorism itself.[28] At the following conference a year later, not a single paper was devoted to terrorism.[29] Academia's rapid descent into irrelevancy has led to the proliferation of both liberal and conservative policy think tanks whose research is eagerly studied by policymakers. Unfortunately, academics are still responsible for educating our youth.

In light of their self-conception as noble dissidents speaking out against an oppressive government, academics have also shown an intolerable contempt for government security agencies, highlighted by boycotts of government programs like the National Security Education Program, which funds students to study regions important to U.S. national security in exchange for a commitment to work in a national security related field.[30]

It may seem that academia is so compromised that there's little hope of recapturing the pre-1960s collegiate spirit of dispassionate inquiry. But the tremendous amount of government funding for higher education—even in ostensibly private schools—provides a mechanism for reform. Universities should have the freedom to publish whatever they want, but the government is under no obligation to fund research that is worthless to the United States or outright hostile to the country. An excellent way to begin reforming academia would be to exert stricter oversight over the Department of Education's Title VI funding program, which doles out over $100 million a year to university area studies programs, mostly on the Middle East. In return for this generous investment of taxpayer dollars, the government largely gets a collection of academic papers that blast the U.S. government for every conceivable crime and "outreach programs" that teach educators how to incorporate multiculturalism and social justice in their instruction.[31]

Previous attempts to reform Title VI have bogged down in Congress due to resistance from the education lobby, which decries every attempt to increase the efficiency of their government subsidies as an intolerable assault on academic freedom. This argument should not even receive a hearing. Academics have no God-given right to federal funding, and the government should not pay for programs that do not further American interests.

Congress's approval in the mid-90s of the Solomon Amendment, which allows the Secretary of Defense to cut off federal funding for universities that ban ROTC or military recruiters, provides a blueprint for action on this issue. Although it hasn't been applied nearly enough—many schools still retain their shameful ban on ROTC—it's been successful when invoked, such as when it forced Harvard Law School to allow access to military recruiters. (This turned out to be quite easy, as Harvard gets 15 percent of its operating budget from federal subsidies.)[32] Notwithstanding their non-stop caterwauling about government oppression, academics would lead much less cozy lives without their lavish government subsidies. So the government should offer universities a new deal: we'll fund what is useful to us, and anything else you can finance yourself.

Countering extremist tendencies and anti-American bias in academia is a daunting undertaking. But the rot in our higher education system—in the humanities in particular—has reached the point of actually undermining our universities' basic educational purpose. Instead of producing well-informed, critical thinking, productive citizens, we are subjecting future generations to a stifling and destructive political dogma that slanders the country that provides access to their education and brazenly insults the military that protects their nation. If the Obama administration is serious about its campaign for "change," academia is a good place to start. If it is not, then opposition Republicans should bring this issue to the full attention of the American people.[33]

★　★　★

THE ROAD AHEAD

"Victory or defeat are things which happen, but duty is a thing which is compulsory and has to go on irrespective, and carries with it its own rewards whatever the upshot of the struggle may be."

Winston Churchill, March 25, 1949

T HE IDEA OF DUTY SEEMS TO HAVE GONE OUT OF STYLE IN RECENT decades. Rather, we live in the golden age of rights. There seems to be no desired thing that is not immediately deemed a right. Free health care? A right. Free education? A right. A comfortable standard of living? A right.

It is a pretty thought that we have a right to whatever we want or need, and that some mysterious force will deliver it. But it is, of course, a fairy tale. History does not disclose any country that thrived based on the entitlements it promised itself. Nations, like people, thrive by imposing duties on themselves.

With envious and emboldened enemies casting their covetous eyes on American power, we citizens of the United States must make as much effort over the next decade to accept duties as we have in the recent past in demanding rights.

It is not just for ourselves that we must sacrifice, but for the universal values America has advocated to the world. Without a strong and dominant America, freedom would have some other national examples, but no effective international champion.

There is a reason that people from across the world still want to come to America and become Americans. It is not just for the jobs and the money. It is for the much sneered at American way of life—that strange combination of self-reliance and community, of freedom and responsibility, of enthusiastic rush into the future and love of tradition, of scientific modernity and deep faith. No other industrial nation is as religious. And no other religious nation is as industrialized.

Until recently, our seeming incongruities have held together, I believe, by virtue of the strong streak of pragmatism that tempers our idealism. Most countries and most cultures tend to lack either pragmatism or idealism. America was born with the magic balance. We had to carve a civilization out of the wilderness—thus our great ideas promptly had to face practical application.

So, for example, in the early nineteenth century we became known as the commercial republic—combining the idealism of representative government with the pragmatism of making a buck. The government offered pragmatic assistance to the private sector without exerting overbearing control, allowing the country to achieve vital national goals like the building of the railroads. Even in what some people view as our imperialistic stage in the latter nineteenth and early twentieth centuries, our foreign ambition was subdued—President McKinley had to be pressured to engage a failing Spain in war. Likewise, when President Teddy Roosevelt launched our Great White Fleet between 1907 and 1909, it showed the flag more than planted it.

Europe, on the other hand, during that period was swept up with the idealism of empire and wasted a fortune grabbing foreign lands.

Lacking American pragmatic restraint (there never was much profit in empire), Europe allowed its imperialistic idealism to drive it into the catastrophe of World War I, and its own destruction. Even as late as the end of World War II, when many urged General Eisenhower to take Berlin before the Soviets did, Ike, a classic American pragmatist, refused. We didn't need the glory of conquering our enemy's capital, so Ike left the Red Army to incur casualties of at least 360,000 troops—and perhaps much more—in the final campaign of the European theater.

Likewise in economic matters, even when America took on the European idea of the welfare state in the twentieth century, we did so with our curious capitalist pragmatism. Europeans consistently viewed our welfare as more stingy than theirs. And it was, but that also left America with a larger private sector that permitted greater economic growth and lower unemployment rates through most of the last half century.

In no area has the American genius for balancing idealism and pragmatism been more clearly revealed than in the mix of the rights and duties of citizenship. Americans have guarded the rights of free speech, religion, bearing arms, due process, and others more tenaciously than have our European cousins. But we have also imposed a greater duty on Americans to fend for ourselves. Our constitution limited the state's economic obligations to those for "the general welfare"—which is to say, programs that benefit everyone, not just a selected class.

Our emphasis on self-sufficiency was balanced by a powerful cultural duty to associate voluntarily in organizations for civic improvement and for charity. Thus, Americans are the world's most generous voluntary donors to charity—on both an absolute and per capita basis. And more than anyone else, we join civic organizations to get things done—from highway beautification to building little league fields to taking care of the homeless. In most other countries, such duties are left to the government.

But in the last decades we've lost this delicate balance. While our sense of duty both to provide for ourselves and to serve our national interest has atrophied, our sense of personal entitlement has dilated.

In the past forty-eight years we have reversed the magnificent proposition of President Kennedy: we can't think of a thing we can do for our country, while we put forward ever growing demands for what our country must do for us.

Not only have we lost the balance between duty and rights, but we are also losing the balance between pragmatism and idealism. On both the left and the right our traditional practical idealism is morphing into rigid ideology, to the detriment of our national interests.

This is evident, for example, in President Obama's fierce commitment to environmentalism—so committed is he that he plans to spend vast sums to subsidize energy sources that are not economically viable, while deliberately hindering the production of coal, natural gas, oil, and nuclear power—the only practical sources of energy.

Likewise, the Democratic Party clings to protectionist dogma to the point that its representatives in Congress oppose free trade agreements with Central America and Columbia. America unambiguously benefits from these pacts, yet Democrats oppose them simply out of ideological stubbornness. Meanwhile, many on the right are no less absolute in their championing of free trade, refusing to acknowledge any faults in our free trade policies, such as cheating by Asian countries that destroys American industries. They have forgotten that Ronald Reagan was a free trader who was pragmatic enough to protect the American car and motorcycle industries from unfair Asian trade practices.

THE COMING STRUGGLE

During the 2008 presidential election, both Barack Obama and John McCain promised to govern in a spirit of bipartisanship. But they missed the point. It will do the country no good if both parties agree to policies that are impractical, ideological, or don't serve the national interest. If the Democrats and Republicans continue to promise the voters even more rights and call for even less exercise of duties, the twenty-first century will see the final decline of American greatness—and with it the best hope for the upward trajectory of civilized life.

As I've argued in this book, President Obama is unlikely to solve the three crucial problems of our time—strengthening the free market economy, improving our national security, and enhancing national unity. But the battle is far from lost, for most Americans still favor a strong, united America and a free economy—however the liberals interpret the outcome of the last election.

During a radio debate shortly after the election, my liberal interlocutor asserted that Obama's victory proved that the public finally had rejected "Reaganism," free markets, and all those religious and cultural arguments that Republicans "have been using to confuse the people."

I disagree. Obama's 53–46 percent win came at a moment of calamitous economic news and a vastly unpopular president. The exit polling disclosed that the public self-identifies as 44 percent moderate, 34 percent conservative, and 22 percent liberal, which was nearly identical to the numbers after Bush's 2004 victory. Moreover, it's a curious fact that 20 percent of self-identified conservatives voted for Obama. Maybe these conservatives were punishing the Republicans, or maybe they just admired Obama personally. Or perhaps they liked his deceptive tax cut promises. Either way, it's too early to declare that this election showed the nation has fundamentally shifted to the left.

But if the Obama team is susceptible to over-interpreting its mandate (as most winners are), conservatives run the risk of underestimating the forces this election unleashed, taking undue comfort in the notion that this still appears to be a center-right nation.

Consider that in 1980, when Ronald Reagan won his first presidential election, the public was self-identified as 46 percent moderate, 28 percent conservative, and 17 percent liberal. By the time Reagan was reelected in 1984, the public had shifted markedly to the right—42 percent moderate, 33 percent conservative and 16 percent liberal. In those four years, Reagan moved 5 percent of the electorate from being moderate to conservative. And that 5 percent has stayed conservative. It is that 5 percent that has made America a center-right country rather than a centrist country—allowing a fairly conservative Republican Party to win congressional and presidential elections most of the time.

That is why it is so vital for both the Republican Party and a newly aroused nationalist/conservative movement to work feverishly during the next four years to make the case to the broadest possible public for our right-of-center views. Obama will try to convert the moderate and conservative voters he won into permanent liberal and moderate voters—just as Reagan did in reverse between 1980 and 1984. If we nationalists and conservatives can make our case, the election of 2008 will be a blip, just a kick-the-bums-out election. But if Obama successfully makes his case to these voters, he could move the center of political gravity to the left for a generation.

COUNTRY BEFORE CREED

Let me close with a vital point. When I call myself a nationalist and propose policies I believe are vital for the strength and freedom of America, I am not suggesting that those who disagree with me are somehow unpatriotic. Quite the contrary. As I described in the first chapter, I started thinking of myself as a nationalist first and a conservative second when I became more aware that America was so vulnerable in the world that American politics can no longer focus on the comparative political advantage of the many factions of our ideological spectrum. Our first thought can no longer be what is best for conservatism, liberalism, Republicans, or Democrats.

The question we must struggle to answer is this: What needs to be done to protect and strengthen our providential nation? Of course, most of the time I will find myself answering that question with a conservative solution, as liberal nationalists (should the breed emerge) will tend toward liberal answers.

But not always. Sometimes, prioritizing our duties over our rights may lead us to a different answer. The very process of asking ourselves first a key question—"Does this proposal strengthen America or not?"—creates a different frame of mind than the questions that most of us ask.

Of course, there are different concepts of what makes America strong. I don't think, for example, that it makes America stronger for the state to spend a quarter million dollars on heroic medical efforts to add a few extra months to the end of my life, if that money would thereby not be available to pay for the fielding of a needed squad of young army infantrymen.

I don't believe that America is stronger if we honor the libertarian principle of opposing the draft, if by doing so we are unable to retain a military large enough to protect our national interests in the world.

I don't believe that America is stronger if we avoid offending every bizarre ideological faction at the price of failing to teach our children the patriotic and glorious history of our nation—and the principles that made us strong and good.

I don't believe that America is stronger if we forego energy independence in hopes of fighting global warming, or if we refuse to provide necessary incentives for the development of oil shale out of an insistence that we adhere to perfect free market principles.

I don't believe that America is stronger if we insist on a democratic election that brings a terrorist group to official government power in the Gaza Strip.

What I do believe—with all the fervor of the immigrant and naturalized American citizen who I am—is this: when America is strong, the hope for individual freedom and human dignity yet lives in the breast of humanity.

★　★　★

ACKNOWLEDGMENTS

I again offer my gratitude to my editor Harry Crocker and all the folks at Regnery. I particularly want to express my deepest appreciation to Jack Langer for his research that made the production of this book possible. I also want to thank the same four of our nine cats—Bosnica, Crooker, Turquoise, and Princess—who sat up with me in my library during the writing of my first book, who have again shrewdly put paws on the delete key at critical moments.

★ ★ ★

NOTES

CHAPTER ONE: THE CASE FOR A NEW AMERICAN NATIONALISM

1 "National Council Report: Sun Setting on the American Century," *The Times*, November 21, 2008, http://www.timesonline.co.uk/tol/news/world/us_and_americas/article5202497.ece.

2 Letter to Horace Greeley, August 22, 1862, reproduced in Harold Holzer and Sara Vaughn Gabbard, eds, *Lincoln and Freedom: Slavery, Emancipation, and the Thirteenth Amendment* (Carbondale: Southern Illinois University Press, 2007), 16.

3 "Rahm Emanuel: Pitbull Politician," *Fortune*, September 26, 2006, http://money.cnn.com/2006/09/17/maga zincs/fortune/politics.fortune/index.htm?postversion=2006092512.

4 *Odyssey*, Chicago Public Radio, http://apps.wbez.org/blog/?p=639.

5 "The history of freedom in Christianity," in *History of Freedom and Other Essays*, 57, as cited in F. A. Hayek, *The Road to Serfdom* (New York: Routledge, 2006), 105.

CHAPTER TWO: BRING BACK THE DRAFT

1   Charles Rangel, "Bring Back the Draft," *New York Times*, December 31, 2002.

2   James W. Geary, *We Need Men: The Union Draft in the Civil War* (DeKalb: Northern Illinois University Press, 1991), 44, 105, 108, 111.

3   Ibid., 173–74.

4   Edward M. Coffman, *The War to End All Wars: The American Military Experience in World War I* (University of Wisconsin Press, 1986), 24–26.

5   Ibid., 28–29.

6   George Q. Flynn, *The Draft, 1940–1973* (Lawrence, KS: University Press of Kansas, 1993), 28, 61, and Lee Kennett, *G.I.: The American Soldier in World War II* (New York: Charles Scribner's Sons, 1987), 5.

7   Kennett, *G.I.*, 15, 17–19.

8   Flynn, *The Draft*, 28, 61.

9   Kennett, *G.I*, 4, 23.

10   Flynn, *The Draft*, 177–78.

11   Michael Foley, *Confronting the War Machine: Draft Resistance During the Vietnam War* (Chapel Hill: University of North Carolina Press, 2003), 6.

12   "Expanding and Funding the Military," editorial, *Washington Times*, January 12, 2007.

13   "The Iraq Surge: Why It's Working," *New York Post*, March 20, 2007.

14   "Baghdadis Enjoy the Moment as Capital Breathes Again," *Financial Times*, December 17, 2007.

15   "Murtha: Surge Is Working; But He Says Iraqis Must Play a Larger Role in Security," *Pittsburgh Post-Gazette*, November 30, 2007.

16   "More Troops Needed Quickly in Afghanistan, General Says," CNN.com, October 1, 2008.

17   "Pentagon Plans to Send More than 12,000 Additional Troops to Afghanistan," *US News and World Report* online, August 19, 2008.

18   "Pentagon Gives Bleak Afghan View," *Wall Street Journal*, September 11, 2008.

19 "Joint Chiefs Advise Change in War Strategy," *Washington Post*, December 14, 2006.

20 William McMichael, "Iraq War has Ground Forces Stretched Thin," *Marine Corps Times*, January 13, 2008.

21 "Army has Record Low Level of Recruits," Breitbart, October 31, 2007.

22 "Army Examines Officer Retention," *Wall Street Journal*, March 26, 2008.

23 Andrew Tilghman, "The Army's Other Crisis," *Washington Monthly*, December 2007.

24 "Gen. McCaffrey on Military Readiness," editorial, *Washington Times*, April 6, 2007, and "Fixing the Guard and Army Reserve," editorial, *Washington Times*, March 7, 2007.

25 Mark Thompson, "Would National Service be Better than the Draft?" *Time*, http://www.time.com/time/specials/2007/article/0,28804,1657256_1657626_1656898-1,00.html.

26 Thomas Donnelly and Frederick Kagan, "We Still Need a Larger Army," *Wall Street Journal*, May 23, 2008.

27 Barack Obama campaign website, http://www.barackobama.com/pdf/issues/Fact_Sheet_Defense_FINAL.pdf.

28 "Is U.S. Ready to Serve?" *Chicago Tribune*, July 3, 2008.

29 Robert Putnam, "Bowling Together," in *United We Serve: National Service and the Future of Citizenship*, ed. E. J. Dionne Jr., Kayla Meltzer Drogosz, and Robert E. Litan (Washington D.C.: Brookings Institution Press, 2003), 13.

30 Kathy Roth-Douquet and Frank Schaeffer, *AWOL: The Unexcused Absence of America's Upper Classes from Military Service—and How It Hurts Our Country* (New York: Collins, 2006), 4–5, 43.

31 Robert Litan makes this point in his essay, "The Obligations of September 11, 2001: The Case for Universal Service," in *United We Serve*, 101.

CHAPTER THREE: AMERICA HELD HOSTAGE

1 Matt Chambers, "What if Iran Blocks the Strait of Hormuz?" *Wall Street Journal*, August 27, 2007

2   http://www.freedomhouse.org/template.cfm?page=138&report=45

3   "World Will struggle to Meet Oil Demand," *Financial Times*, October 28, 2008.

4   Michael T. Klare, *Resource Wars: The New Landscape of Global Conflict* (New York: Henry Holt and Company, 2001), 25.

5   "Chavez Pushes Petro-Diplomacy," *Washington Post*, November 22, 2005.

6   "Venezuela's Oil Based Economy," *Council on Foreign Relations*, November 27, 2006, http://www.cfr.org/publication/12089/venezuelas_oilbased_economy.html.

7   "Hugo's Arms Spree," *New York Post*, August 7, 2008, http://www.nypost.com/seven/08072008/postopinion/opedcolumnists/hugos_arms_spree_123385.htm.

8   "Venezuela Rivals U.S. in Aid to Bolivia," *New York Times*, February 23, 2007.

9   "Castro's Exit Puts Chavez on Center Stage," *Wall Street Journal*, February 21, 2008.

10   "Chavez Pushes Petro-Diplomacy," *Washington Post*, November 22, 2005.

11   "Colombia is Flashpoint in Chavez's Feud with U.S.," *New York Times* website, March 5, 2008, http://www.nytimes.com/2008/03/05/world/americas/05venez.html?pagewanted=1&ref=world.

12   "$32Bln Fund Must Go the Extra Mile," editorial, *Moscow Times*, February 4, 2008.

13   "Turning Russia into a Global Citizen," *Moscow Times*, October 27, 2008.

14   "Russian Energy Deal Adds to Europe Fears," http://www.msnbc.msn.com/id/22848715/, Jan 26, 2008.

15   "A Bear at the Throat," *The Economist*, April 12, 2007.

16   http://www.timesonline.co.uk/tol/news/world/europe/article4508590.ece

17   National Security Consequences of U.S. Oil Dependency: Report of an Independent Task Force. Council on Foreign Relations, 2006, 18, 19.

18   Klare, *Resource Wars*.

CHAPTER FOUR: MAKING AMERICA ENERGY INDEPENDENT

1   "Surging Costs of Groceries Hits Home," *Boston Globe* online, March 9, 2008, http://www.boston.com/business/personalfinance/articles/2008/03/09/surging_costs_of_groceries_hit_home/?page=1.

2   "Secret Report: Biofuel Caused Food Crisis," *The Guardian*, July 4, 2008.

3   "U.N. Says Biofuel Subsidies Raise Food Bill and Hunger," *New York Times*, October 8, 2008.

4   Robert Bryce, "Corn Dog: The Ethanol Subsidy Is Worse than You Can Imagine," *Slate*, http://www.slate.com/id/2122961/.

5   George Will, "The Biofuel Follies," *Newsweek*, February 11, 2008.

6   Barack Obama campaign website, http://www.barackobama.com/pdf/factsheet_energy_speech_080308.pdf.

7   "Millions More Face Relocation From Three Gorges Reservoir Area," Xinhua News Agency, http://news.xinhuanet.com/english/2007-10/11/content_6864252.htm.

8   Jessee H. Ausubel, "Renewable and Nuclear Heresies," *International Journal of Nuclear Governance, Economy and Ecology*, Vol. 1, No. 3, July 24, 2007, 229–43.

9   Jerry Taylor, "Alternative Energy in the Dock," CATO Institute, http://www.cato.org/pubs/articles/taylor-poweringamerica.pdf.

10   "Oil Billionaire Revises Plan to Reduce Foreign Oil Imports," *Arizona Republic*, November 12, 2008, http://www.azcentral.com/arizonarepublic/business/articles/2008/11/12/20081112biz-pickens1112.html.

11   Jonathan Rauch, "Electro-Shock Therapy," *The Atlantic*, July/August 2008, http://www.theatlantic.com/doc/200807/general-motors, and Holman W. Jenkins, Jr., "Obama's Car Puzzle," *Wall Street Journal*, November 12, 2008, and "Will the Chevy Volt Save the World?" *Fortune* magazine, September 23, 2008, http://money.cnn.com/2008/09/22/news/companies/taylor_volt.fortune/index.htm?postversion=2008092309. .

12   "National Security," 15.

13   Barack Obama campaign website, http://my.barackobama.com/page/
      content/newenergy_more#relief.

14   "Communists, Oil and the Florida Coast," *Washington Times*, edi-
      torial, May 4, 2006.

15   "Report to Congress: Comprehensive Inventory of U.S. OCS Oil and
      Natural Gas Resources," Minerals Management Service, February 2006.

16   "Obama Signals Support for Wider Off-Shore Drilling," *Washington
      Post*, August 2, 2008.

17   Newt Gingrich and Vince Haley, *Drill Here, Drill Now, Pay Less*
      (Regnery Publishing: Washington, D.C., 2008), 87–91.

18   "Arctic National Wildlife Refuge, 1002 Area, Petroleum Assessment,
      1998, Including Economic Analysis," U.S. Geological Survey,
      http://pubs.usgs.gov/fs/fs-0028-01/fs-0028-01.htm.

19   "Communists, Oil and the Florida Coast," *Washington Times*, edi-
      torial, May 4, 2006.

20   "Oil Shale: History, Incentives and Policy," *Congressional Research
      Service*, April 13, 2006.

21   Ibid.

22   "Careful Steps on Colo. Shale," *Denver Post*, editorial, June 1, 2006.

23   "America's Strategic Unconventional Fuels, Vol II," *Task Force on
      Strategic Unconventional Fuels*, September 2007.

24   "Oil Shale Development in the United States: Prospects and Policy
      Issues," RAND Corporation, 2005, http://rand.org/pubs/monographs/
      2005/RAND_MG414.pdf.

25   Official   website   of   Senator   Jim   DeMint,
      http://demint.senate.gov/public/index.cfm?FuseAction=JimsJournal.
      Detail&Blog_ID=9a2397c9-e8a5-2da3-c8a3-2cd5fe8fa96b.

26   "Activists May Sue DOI for Violating FLMPA in Drafting Oil Shale
      Rule," *EnergyWashington Week*, October 15, 2008.

27   Bjørn Lomborg, *Cool It* (New York: Alfred A. Knopf, 2008), 41.

28   "Ted Turner: Global Warming Could Lead to Cannibalism," *Atlanta
      Journal-Constitution*, April 3, 2008, http://www.ajc.com/metro/
      content/news/stories/2008/04/03/turner_0404.html.

29   Barack Obama campaign website, http://www.barackobama.com/
      pdf/issues/EnvironmentFactSheet.pdf.

30   "Climate Issues & Questions," *The Marshall Institute*, 2006, 17–18.

31   "The Mystery of Global Warming's Missing Heat," NPR website, http://www.npr.org/templates/story/story.php?storyId=88520025.

32   "Global Temperatures to 'Decrease,'" *BBC News*, http://news.bbc.co.uk/2/hi/science/nature/7329799.stm.

33   Singer and Avery, *Unstoppable Global Warming*, 1–11.

34   Lomborg, *Cool It,* 38–39.

35   Robert F. Kennedy, Jr., "For They That Sow the Wind Shall Reap the Whirlwind," *The Huffington Post*, http://www.huffingtonpost.com/robert-f-kennedy-jr/for-they-that-sow-the-_b_6396.html.

36   Al Gore interview, *60 Minutes*, March 30, 2008.

37   William D. Nordhaus and Joseph Boyer, *Warming the World: Economic Models of Global Warming* (Cambridge, Mass: MIT Press, 2000), 161–62.

38   Lomborg, *Cool It*, 9, 22, 33, 41, 162.

39   Clive Crook, "Sins of Emission," *Atlantic Monthly*, April 2008.

40   "Hard Truths, Executive Summary," *National Petroleum Council*, July 2007.

41   "On the Trail/Dirty Politics; A Coal-Fired Squabble," *Los Angeles Times*, November 3, 2008.

42   "The Plowboy Interview," *Mother Earth News*, November/December 1977, http://www.motherearthnews.com/Do-It-Yourself/1977-11-01/Plowboy-Interview.aspx?page=14.

43   Paul Ehrlich, "An Ecologist's Perspective on Nuclear Power," Federal Academy of Science Public Issue Report, May–June 1975, cited in Jerry Taylor, "Energy Conservation and Efficiency: The Case Against Coercion," *The Cato Institute*, http://www.cato.org/pubs/pas/pa-189.html.

44   "Frequently Asked Questions - Three Mile Island Accident - March 28, 1979," *American Nuclear Society*, http://www.ans.org/pi/resources/sptopics/tmi/faq.html.

45   "Chernobyl's Legacy: Health, Environmental, and Socio-Environmental Impacts," *The Chernobyl Forum*, http://www.iaea.org/Publications/ Booklets/Chernobyl/chernobyl.pdf.

46   Greenpeace website, http://www.greenpeace.org/usa/news/american-chernobyl-report.

47   Barack Obama campaign website, http://www.barackobama.com/pdf/factsheet_energy_speech_080308.pdf.

CHAPTER FIVE: IN PRAISE OF CENSORSHIP

1   Jeff Jacoby, "About our 'Dictator,'" *Boston Globe*, July 5, 2006.

2   Joe Conason, *It Can Happen Here* (New York: Thomas Dunne Books, 2007), 9.

3   Marc Sageman, *Leaderless Jihad* (Philadelphia: University of Pennsylvania Press, 2008), 148–50.

4   "Nuclear Attack on D.C. a Hypothetical Disaster," *Washington Times*, April 16, 2008.

5   Corruption Perceptions Index 2007, *Transparency International*, http://www.transparency.org/policy_research/surveys_indices/cpi/2007.

6   "Mass Transit System Threat Assessment," Transportation Security Administration,   February   29,   2008, http://msnbcmedia.msn.com/i/msnbc/sections/tvnews/masstransitsystemthreatassessment.pdf.

7   Richard A. Posner, *Not a Suicide Pact* (Oxford and New York: Oxford University Press, 206), 6.

8   William H. Rehnquist, *All the Laws But One* (New York: Vintage Books, 1998), 222–23.

9   Posner, *Not a Suicide Pact*, 40, 44.

10   Geoffrey R. Stone, *Perilous Times* (New York and London: W.W. Norton & Company, 2004), 252–83.

11   Tony Blankley, *The West's Last Chance* (Washington, D.C.: Regnery Publishing, 2005), 116–17.

12   Mahmoud al-Zahar, "No Peace Without Hamas," *Washington Post*, April 17, 2008, and Mousa Abu Marzook, "What Hamas is Seeking," *Washington Post*, January 31, 2006.

13   http://newsweek.washingtonpost.com/onfaith/muslims_speak_out/2007/07/sayyed_fadlallah.html.

14   The *Washington Post* itself first reported that Fadlallah was a suspect in the barracks bombing. See "Sheik With Iranian Ties Is Suspect in Bombings," *Washington Post*, October 28, 1983. Later, in May 1985, the paper ran a column casting doubt on the source of the U.S. intelligence reports of Fadlallah's involvement. However, the column makes clear that by that time, the U.S. had other, independent sources testifying to Fadlallah's role in the bombing. See David B. Ottaway, "News Analysis; Conclusive Proof of Terrorist Acts By Car-Bomb Target Is Not Evident," *Washington Post*, May 17, 1985. For an excellent account of Fadlallah's murky history and connections to Hezbollah, see Martin Kramer's two-part essay, "The Oracle of Hizbullah: Sayyid Muhammad Husayn Fadlallah," http://www.geocities.com/martinkramerorg/Oracle1.htm and http://www.geocities.com/martinkramerorg/Oracle2.htm.

15   "A Wake-Up Vote in the House," editorial, *New York Times*, June 17, 2005.

16   Conason, *It Can Happen Here*, 95.

17   Jonah Goldberg, *Liberal Fascism* (New York and London: Doubleday, 2007), 112.

18   Thomas J. DiLorenzo, *The Real Lincoln* (New York: Three Rivers Press, 2003), 138–45.

19   Michelle Malkin, *In Defense of Internment* (Washington, D.C.: Regnery Publishing, 2004), 82–83.

20   David B. Rivkin Jr. & Lee A. Casey, "A Key Tool Salvaged?" *National Review Online*, February 2, 2007, http://article.nationalreview.com/?q=NTkwZWQ1ZjEwZWM1MWY1NWVlNGU0NWY5ZWNkZDM5N2M=.

21   "Nomination in Hand, Obama Stiffs the Dem Left on Fisa Vote," *L.A. Times* blog, http://latimesblogs.latimes.com/washington/2008/07/obama-fisa.html.

22   "Surveillance Disclosure Denounced; 'Disgraceful,' Says Bush of Reports," *Washington Post*, June 27, 2006.

23   "Letter From Bill Keller on the *Times*'s Banking Records Report," *New York Times*, June 25, 2006.

24 "Surveillance Disclosure Denounced," *Washington Post*, June 27, 2006.

25 "Qaeda Goes Dark After a U.S. Slip," *New York Sun*, October 9, 2007, http://www2.nysun.com/foreign/qaeda-goes-dark-after-a-us-slip/.

26 "Rove Fight Escalates," *Washington Times*, July 15, 2005.

27 "Weighing the Risks," *New York Times*, July 6, 2008.

CHAPTER SIX: A LAW CODE FOR WARTIME

1 Malkin, *In Defense of Internment* (Washington, D.C.: Regnery Publishing, 2004), 86.

2 Thomas dissent, *Hamdan* v. *Rumsfeld*, 548 U.S. 557 (2006), http://www.law.cornell.edu/supct/html/05-184.ZD1.html.

3 Scalia dissent, *Boumediene* v. *Bush*, http://www.law.cornell.edu/supct/html/06-1195.ZD1.html.

4 Andrew C. McCarthy, *Willful Blindness* (New York and London: Encounter Books, 2008), 304–05.

5 Ibid., 312.

6 "Obama Says Gitmo Facility Should Close," *Washington Post*, June 24, 2007.

7 "Transcript: Jake Tapper Interviews Barack Obama," ABC News, June 16, 2008, http://abcnews.go.com/WN/Politics/Story?id=5178123&page=1.

8 "Next President Will Face Test on Detainees," *New York Times*, November 2, 2008.

9 "Intelligence Policy to Stay Largely Intact," *Wall Street Journal*, November 11, 2008.

10 One of the fifteen applicants was apparently initially rejected and allowed to resubmit his application, which was then approved. Joel Mowbray, "Visas that Should have been Denied," *National Review Online*, October 9, 2002, http://www.nationalreview.com/mowbray/mowbray100902.asp.

11 Joel Mowbray, "Open Door for Saudi Terrorists," *National Review Online*, June 14, 2002, http://www.nationalreview.com/mowbray/mowbray061402.asp.

12 "Senators Question 'Phoenix Memo' Author," CNN, May 21, 2002, http://archives.cnn.com/2002/US/05/21/phoenix.memo/index.html.

13 *The 9/11 Commission Report* (USA: W. W. Norton & Company, 1994), 272, 347.

14 McCarthy, *Willful Blindness*, 90.

15 "'Jihadist' Booted from Government Lexicon," *Associated Press*, http://ap.google.com/article/ALeqM5i3X6Gha4z-MCq9pU0vC4FWqDCXrwD908CUGO0.

16 "Feds Defend Partnership with Islamic Group Under Scrutiny," *Cybercast News Service*, January 16, 2007, http://www.cnsnews.com/ViewNation.asp?Page=/Nation/archive/200701/NAT20070116a.html.

17 Robert Spencer, *Stealth Jihad* (Washington, D.C.: Regncry Publishing, 2008), 107–08.

18 Debra Burlingame, "On a Wing and a Prayer," *Wall Street Journal*, December 6, 2006, http://www.opinionjournal.com/editorial/feature.html?id=110009348.

19 "Libel Without Borders," *New York Times*, October 7, 2007.

20 "Governor Paterson Signs Legislation Protecting New Yorkers Against Infringement of First Amendment Rights by Foreign Libel Judgments," New York Governor website, http://www.ny.gov/governor/press/press_0501082.html.

21 These cases and many others are catalogued in Robert Spencer's *Stealth Jihad*.

22 "A Brutal Beating and Justice Meted Out in a Humble Back Street Café: How Sharia Law Already Operates in Britain," *Daily Mail*, February 10, 2008, http://www.dailymail.co.uk/pages/live/articles/news/news.html?in_article_id=513218&in_page_id=1770.

23 "Sharia Law Already Enforced in 10 Courts," *Daily Telegraph*, February 9, 2008, and "Sharia Law Is Spreading as the Authority of British Justice Wanes," *Daily Telegraph*, November 29, 2006.

24   "Revealed: UK's First Official Sharia Courts," *The Sunday Times (London)*, September 14, 2008.

25   "Sharia-Compliant Mortgages," BBC website, http://www.bbc.co.uk/religion/religions/islam/living/mortgages.shtml.

26   "Islamic Law to 'Influence UK System,'" *The Herald* (Scotland), May 23, 2008, http://www.theherald.co.uk/news/news/display.var.2272176.0.islamic_law_to_influence_uk_system.php. [1]

CHAPTER SEVEN: PUTTING AMERICA'S INTERESTS FIRST

1   Full transcript, Saddleback Presidential Forum, http://www.clipsandcomment.com/2008/08/17/full-transcript-saddle-back-presidential-forum-sen-barack-obama-john-mccain-moderated-by-rick-warren/.

2   http://www.whitehouse.gov/inaugural/

3   Henry A. Kissinger, "Iraq and Phase II," *Washington Post*, January 13, 2002, and Tony Blankley, "War Comes Closer; A Period of 'Measureless Peril' Could be in the Offing," *Washington Times*, August 14, 2002.

4   "The Foreign Policy Race; Madeleine Albright's Audition," *New York Times*, September 22, 1996.

5   Barack Obama campaign website, http://origin.barackobama.com/issues/iraq/.

6   Barack Obama, "Renewing American Leadership," *Foreign Affairs*, July/August 2007.

7   Barack Obama campaign website, http://origin.barackobama.com/issues/foreign_policy/#iran.

8   Ibid., http://origin.barackobama.com/issues/foreign_policy/#iran.

9   Ron Paul, *The Revolution: A Manifesto* (New York and Boston: Grand Central Publishing, 2008), 37.

10   Pat Buchanan, *Churchill, Hitler, and the "Unnecessary War": How Britain Lost its Empire and the West Lost the World* (New York: Crown Publishers, 2008).

11   "Russian Defense Budget May Rise 25 Percent in 2009," Associated Press, September 19, 2008.

12 "Nato Rapid Response Unit Proposed to Address Fears About Russia," *LA Times*, September 19, 2008.

13 Ibid.

14 "Supreme Court Overrules Bush, OKs Texas Execution," CNN.com, http://edition.cnn.com/2008/CRIME/03/25/scotus.texas/.

15 Ibid.

16 Barack Obama, "Renewing American Leadership," *Foreign Affairs*, July/August 2007.

17 Jonah Goldberg, "Europe's Canary in a Coal Mine?" *National Review Online*, October 10, 2007.[1]

CHAPTER EIGHT: BROADCASTING LIBERTY

1 U.S. Department of Defense, "National Defense Strategy," June 2008.

2 Daniel Kimmage and Kathleen Ridolfo, "Iraq Insurgent Media: The War of Images and Ideas," Radio Fee Europe/Radio Liberty, June 2007.

3 Dr. Carnes Lord and Helle Dale, "Public Diplomacy and the Cold War: Lessons learned," The Heritage Foundation, September 18 2007.

4 "Address of the President of the Czech Republic Vaclav Havel," Vaclav Havel official website, May 4, 2001, http://www.vaclavhavel.cz/showtrans.php?cat=projevy&val=48_aj_p rojevy.html&typ=HTML.

5 "Muslim Public Opinion on US Policy," World Public Opinion, http://www.worldpublicopinion.org/pipa/pdf/apr07/START_Apr07_r pt.pdf.

CHAPTER NINE: BACK TO BASICS: READING, WRITING, AND ROTC

1 Larry Schweikart, *48 Liberal Lies About American History* (New York: Sentinel, 2008), 239.

2 "World History Textbooks: A Review," American Textbook Council, 2004, p 20, http://www.historytextbooks.org/worldhistory.pdf.

3 Ibid., 24.

4 Lynn Cheney, "The End of History," *Wall Street Journal*, October 20, 1994.

5   Gary Tobin and Dennis Ybarra, *The Trouble with Textbooks* (Lanham: Lexington Books, 2008), 15.

6   Ibid., 29.

7   Ibid., 29, 82–85

8   Sol Stern, "The Ed Schools' Latest—and Worst—Humbug," *City Journal*, Summer 2006, http://www.city-journal.org/html/16_3_ed_school.html.

9   "Support Bill Ayers," http://www.supportbillayers.org/.

10   "Ayers Reflects on Obama in New Afterward to Memoir," Associated Press, November 14, 2008.

11   "Social Justice Mission Statement," American Educational Research Association, https://www.aera.net/AboutAERA/Default.aspx?menu_id=90&id=1960.

12   Michael Knox Beran, "Self-reliance vs. Self-esteem," *City Journal*, Winter 2004, http://www.city-journal.org/html/14_1_self_reliance.html.

13   Thomas Sowell, *Inside American Education* (New York and London: Free Press, 1993).

14   George Will, "Teaching 9/11 Lies," *Jewish World Review*, August 26, 2002, http://www.jewishworldreview.com/cols/will082602.asp.

15   For an excellent argument for teaching patriotism, see Bill Bennett, *The Educated Child* (New York and London: Simon & Schuster, 1999), 191–92.

16   Barack Obama, campaign website, http://www.barackobama.com/pdf/issues/PreK-12EducationFactSheet.pdf.

17   Stanley Kurtz, "Obama and Ayers Pushed Radicalism on Schools," *Wall Street Journal*, September 23, 2008.

18   Barack Obama campaign website, http://www.barackobama.com/pdf/NationalServicePlanFactSheet.pdf.

19   "Junior ROTC Takes a Hit in LA," *Los Angeles Times*, February 19, 2007.

20   Ibid.

21   "College Faculties a Most Liberal Lot, Study Finds," *Washington Post*, March 29, 2005.

22   For an insider's account of Black Panther crimes under the leadership of Elaine Brown, see David Horowitz, *Radical Son* (New York: The Free Press, 1997).

23   "Baruch Disses Freshman Academic Freedom," American Council of Trustees and Alumni, http://www.goactablog.org/blog/archives/2006/08/.

24   "University of Delaware Requires Students to Undergo Ideological Reeducation," Foundation for Individual Rights in Education, http://www.thefire.org/index.php/article/8555.html, and "Excerpts from University of Delaware Office of Residency Life Diversity Facilitation Training," Foundation for Individual Rights in Education, http://www.thefire.org/index.php/article/8552.html.

25   For an account of the water buffalo case written by the student's faculty advocate, who went on to co-found FIRE, read Alan Charles Kors, *The Shadow University* (New York: Free Press, 1998).

26   "Speech Code of the Month: University of the Pacific," Foundation for Individual Rights in Education, http://www.thefirc.org.

27   For a sampling of such stories catalogued by FIRE, go to http://www.thefire.org/index.php/search/results/?cx=0009612331299 80584517%3Ailyoribxziu&cof=FORID%3A11&q=affirmative 1 action 1 bakesale&sa.x=17&sa.y=11#1169.

28   Jonathan Calt Harris, "Academia Silent on Militant Islam," Frontpagemag, http://frontpagemag.com/Articles/Printable.aspx?GUID=8DE519D4-18A1-4793-BABB-83778A583C42.

29   Jonathan Calt Harris, "The Middle East Studies Left," Frontpagemag, http://frontpagemag.com/Articles/Printable.asp?ID=10664.

30   Stanley Kurtz, "Boycott Exposure," *National Review Online*, April 1, 2004, http://nationalreview.com/kurtz/kurtz200404010914.asp.

31   For a comprehensive critique on Middle Eastern studies, see Martin Kramer, *Ivory Towers on Sand* (Washington D.C.: Washington Institute for Near East Policy, 2001).

32   "Letter from Dean Kagan on Military Recruiting," http://www.law.harvard.edu/news/2005/09/20_recruiting.php.

★ ★ ★

INDEX